D0901592

Included in the series:*

* Also published in French. Other titles to appear.

Early childhood education: need and opportunity

David P. Weikart

Paris 2000
UNESCO: International Institute for Educational Planning

The Swedish International Development Co-operation Agency (Sida)
has provided financial assistance for the publication of this booklet.

Published in 2000 by the United Nations
Educational, Scientific and Cultural Organization
7 place de Fontenoy, F 75352 Paris 07 SP
Printed in France by SAGIM
Cover design by Pierre Finot

Fundamentals of educational planning

The booklets in this series are written primarily for two types of clientele: those engaged in educational planning and administration, in developing as well as developed countries; and others, less specialized, such as senior government officials and policy-makers who seek a more general understanding of educational planning and of how it is related to overall national development. They are intended to be of use either for private study or in formal training programmes.

Since this series was launched in 1967 practices and concepts of educational planning have undergone substantial change. Many of the assumptions which underlay earlier attempts to rationalize the process of educational development have been criticized or abandoned. Even if rigid mandatory centralized planning has now clearly proven to be inappropriate, this does not mean that all forms of planning have been dispensed with. On the contrary, the need for collecting data, evaluating the efficiency of existing programmes, undertaking a wide range of studies, exploring the future and fostering broad debate on these bases to guide educational policy and decision-making has become even more acute than before. One cannot make sensible policy choices without assessing the present situation, specifying the goals to be reached, marshalling the means to attain them and monitoring what has been accomplished. Hence planning is also a way to organize learning: by mapping, targeting, acting and correcting.

The scope of educational planning has been broadened. In addition to the formal system of education, it is now applied to all other important educational efforts in non-formal settings. Attention to the growth and expansion of education systems is being complemented and sometimes even replaced by a growing concern for the quality of the entire educational process and for the control of its results. Finally, planners and administrators have become more and more aware of the importance of implementation strategies and of the role of different regulatory mechanisms in this respect: the choice of financing methods, the examination and certification procedures

5

or various other regulation and incentive structures. The concern of planners is twofold: to reach a better understanding of the validity of education in its own empirically observed specific dimensions and to help in defining appropriate strategies for change.

The purpose of these booklets includes monitoring the evolution and change in educational policies and their effect upon educational planning requirements; highlighting current issues of educational planning and analyzing them in the context of their historical and societal setting; and disseminating methodologies of planning which can be applied in the context of both the developed and the developing countries.

For policy-making and planning, vicarious experience is a potent source of learning: the problems others face, the objectives they seek, the routes they try, the results they arrive at and the unintended results they produce are worth analysis.

In order to help the Institute identify the real up-to-date issues in educational planning and policy-making in different parts of the world, an Editorial Board has been appointed, composed of two general editors and associate editors from different regions, all professionals of high repute in their own field. At the first meeting of this new Editorial Board in January 1990, its members identified key topics to be covered in the coming issues under the following headings:

1. Education and development.
2. Equity considerations.
3. Quality of education.
4. Structure, administration and management of education.
5. Curriculum.
6. Cost and financing of education.
7. Planning techniques and approaches.
8. Information systems, monitoring and evaluation.

Each heading is covered by one or two associate editors.

The series has been carefully planned but no attempt has been made to avoid differences or even contradictions in the views expressed by the authors. The Institute itself does not wish to impose any official doctrine. Thus, while the views are the responsibility of the authors and may not always be shared by UNESCO or the IIEP, they warrant attention in the international forum of ideas. Indeed, one of the purposes of this series is to reflect a diversity of experience and opinions by giving different authors from a wide range of backgrounds and disciplines the opportunity of expressing their views on changing theories and practices in educational planning.

Providing quality early childhood care and development programmes is a challenge for policy makers and educational planners all over the world. For many years education was thought to begin in school, at the primary education level. Pre-school was considered a luxury available in those countries or for those families who could afford it. Indeed pre-school education developed in industrialized countries as a result of the increase in female participation in the labour force. As women increasingly integrated into the workforce in industry and services, pre-school provision expanded as a child-care mechanism for younger and younger children. The potential of such programmes for the psychosocial development and learning of children was soon discovered, and early childhood care and education are part of many compensatory programmes in developed countries.

This booklet, by David Weikart, presents the organizational arrangements of pre-school education in a number of developed and developing countries. It also clearly demonstrates the short- and long-term effects of early childhood education programmes for the psychological development and future learning of children; particularly those from disadvantaged backgrounds. It is, therefore, of great relevance to planners and decision-makers concerned with providing quality early childhood education the world over. While this publication focuses primarily on OECD countries, another will pay particular attention to the needs of resource-poor countries, where programmes might have to be constructed in other, more innovative, ways, relying heavily on local resources and communities.

The Institute is very grateful to Mr Weikart, President of the High/Scope Educational Research Foundation, for this essential and comprehensive document. We are also grateful to Professor Postlethwaite who directed its preparation.

Gudmund Hernes
Director, IIEP

Preface

The field of early childhood education has expanded rapidly in the last decade of the 20th century. As more and more women have entered the workforce so have more very young children been placed outside the home for care and education. The settings in which very young children are placed vary considerably from actually being at home with the family to being 'minded' by a person nearby to being placed in a private institution or in one run by the State. In some countries more than 80 per cent of an age group of three year-olds are in pre-school education. Even in some not so industrialized countries there are 30 and 40 per cent of children in early childhood educational settings.

But what is known about the forms of early childhood care and education? To what extent do they differ given that the cultures in which such education takes place differ a lot? How effective is early childhood education? Are there any advantages for those children attending early education compared to those not doing so? What is the sort of information that educational planners responsible for early childhood education and decision-makers need to have?

What do teachers think that these young children should learn? What do the parents actually want the children to learn? Is there agreement between teachers and parents on what the children should learn? How can high quality programmes be created? What sorts of health and safety standards are needed? What sorts of persons should be recruited for staff positions in these programmes? How should they be trained? What kinds of auxiliary services are needed, if any? Are there model programmes that are worthy of consideration?

The IIEP has been lucky in persuading David Weikart to write this short booklet for educational planners and other interested people. David Weikart is the head of High/Scope Educational Research Foundation in Ypsilanti, Michigan, USA. He has spent more than thirty years in the field of early childhood research. Two of his most important studies have been:

(a) a follow-up study in the United States to study the effects of pre-school education on later development in children, and (b) an international study in several countries to examine the different types of settings in early childhood education and care and the effect of these settings on the development of children. In this booklet, Dr Weikart has produced a summary of results of these studies that are relevant for educational planners.

There is an enormous challenge for those in charge of early childhood education and care in ensuring that provision is relevant and of high quality. The author has shown that there are several advantages to having early childhood education: it helps overcome social disadvantage; it also has, on average, positive long-term effects for all having undergone early childhood programmes compared with those not having attended such programmes. This booklet provides the kinds of issues that have to be taken into account when planning this kind of education.

T. Neville Postlethwaite
Co-General Editor

Contents

11

Introduction

The topic of early childhood care and education was not on the public policy agenda 15, or even 10, years ago. Suddenly two major forces have converged to bring it to the attention of governments and social planners throughout the world. First, women are entering the paid workforce in increasing numbers in almost every country. This trend is the result of families' mass movement to the cities and away from subsistence farming in developing countries and also of better education and improved opportunities for women in developed countries. But when women are in the paid workforce, what happens to the children? Second, long-term and well-documented studies of the impact of early childhood care and education have reported significant benefits for disadvantaged youngsters who have the opportunity to participate in high-quality programmes. Carefully controlled studies, such as the High/Scope Perry Pre-school Project in the USA, have found that poor children participating in pre-school programmes show long-term improvements lasting into adulthood. And these improvements relate to matters of significant public concern, such as reducing crime, increasing employment and improving family stability. To meet the child-care needs of families with both parents in the labour force (or engaged in furthering their education), and to act on the evidence that society as a whole can benefit from the provision of high-quality early education programmes, many countries around the world are now giving much-needed attention to providing early childhood services.

This monograph examines early childhood care and education from a variety of perspectives. The first chapter looks at early childhood care and education from an historical perspective. It includes short summaries of the evolution of services in two countries. These summaries have been adapted from profiles prepared for a pre-primary study sponsored by the International Association for the Evaluation of Educational Achievement (called the IEA Pre-primary Project). The High/Scope Educational Research Foundation is the

International Co-ordinating Centre for this study. The short history in Chapter 1 provides a context for the information presented in the rest of the monograph, including news about the many changes that have most recently occurred in the early childhood picture.

Today, there is much talk about the need for early childhood care and education, but to what extent are pre-primary services actually used in various countries? This topic is discussed in Chapter 2, where 21,545 families in 11 countries who participated in the IEA Pre-primary Project's household survey indicate their service usage. The sample for the study was randomly selected from urban and rural areas to represent the country as a whole. Important for national planning is the information this survey uncovered about the extent and type of service usage and satisfaction with services. But it is the task of Chapter 3 to give information about what teachers and families actually expect children to learn in their out-of-home programmes. When children spend significant time away from the family during these critical developmental years, what happens to them is important to their parents; it is also important to the society at large, for the society depends on the family (and now on the family's surrogates) to prepare citizens for the community. We already know much about what families can do towards this end. What can child-care and education centres, with groups of unrelated children and paid caregivers and teachers, accomplish?

Fortunately, there is a growing body of evidence about the impact care and education outside the home can have on children. There is also information about what may be the best ages at which to provide such services if funding for them is limited. Chapter 4 looks at pre-school programmes and possible choices regarding their content. Of special importance in the chapter is the report of findings from the High/Scope Perry Pre-school study in the USA after more than two decades of follow-up of its pre-school participants. Policy-makers rarely have recourse to such a tightly controlled study, conducted over a long duration, demonstrating such a positive impact. However, Chapter 5 cautions that not just any pre-school programme will provide the return on investment found in the High/Scope Perry study. Various model curriculum programmes are available. Among these, the one that seems most logical to most non-early childhood educators is the approach that teaches young children the facts they will need to be successful in later schooling. Yet the data point the opposite way, indicating that successful early childhood care and education respect the unique developmental level of the child, by recognizing the child's need to initiate and actively construct knowledge. These are the kinds of experiences required to lay the foundation. The roof of the building may be made of asphalt shingle, thatch or clay tile, but the foundation certainly is not.

The sixth chapter is focused on the criteria for selecting an effective curriculum and the importance of training staff (teachers and other adults) to use the curriculum approach. When little was known about the impact of early childhood care and education, or when service provision was primarily for children's health (physical or mental) or safety, little thought was given to what processes were actually used with children. Now it is different: great skill is essential, and our responsibility is clear: programmes must provide adequately trained and supervised staff to accomplish their potential with children.

The final chapter looks at some of the major issues involved in planning and operating effective early childhood programmes.

I. Early childhood education: a short history

In most countries, early childhood care and education as known today, are of fairly recent development. Various histories of early childhood education (e.g. Cleverley and Phillips, 1986; Osborn, 1991) illustrate the extent to which children, especially girls, were often regarded as liabilities and subjected to indifference instead of nurturing. Indeed, only in the 1900s were such general practices as infanticide by exposure, or the more genteel form of discarding infants called 'potting' (which the infant Moses experienced), called into question. Disposing of children in these ways was finally accepted as illegal, and governments attempted to reduce the practice. However, problems still exist in some areas of the world, though the forms of rejection or neglect now differ. Gender selection through abortion occurs in many countries. Infant girls and handicapped children are still subject to neglect and indifference. Child prostitution and child slavery still exist.

During earlier periods, child labour was valued in industrial areas and on farms. While often horrendous, the conditions of child labour were frequently better than the squalor and poverty in which the vast majority of families lived. But in the 1800s, a number of French (Marbeau in 1844) and German (Oberlin in 1799, Pestalozzi in 1801, Froebel in 1837) reformers began to understand the process of child growth and development. They began to sense that childhood is different from adulthood and that children are not just miniature adults. Pioneers such as Froebel, starting in 1837, and the McMillan sisters, starting in 1913, began to make an impact on actual programmes for large numbers of children.

In the book *How nations serve young children*, Olmstedt and Weikart (1989) brought together the histories of early childhood in 14 countries, ranging from Nigeria to China to Germany. It is clear from each of these histories that the modern thrust of early childhood care and education has been evident only since the post-Second World

War period. However, the current state of early childhood care and education has evolved in a step-by-step process over many years in most of these countries. (See, for example, *Box 1* below describing the process in China and Nigeria.)

In the USA, real change came in the 1950s with the growing awareness that something needed to be done for children with special education needs. The focus was initially on the handicapped, but it was quickly extended to impoverished children, in the 1960s, when the awareness of civil rights issues spread into education. Terms such as 'culturally deprived' were used in the early 1960s, before the advent of Head Start. [Initiated by President Lyndon B. Johnson in 1965 as part of his great society war on poverty programmes, Head Start was created to provide a range of health, social and educational services to both disadvantaged children and their families. The programme in 1999 served 798,000 children with an annual budget of US$4 billion.] As people realized that the problems of these children were the result of poverty and social indifference to their culture and needs, the term 'culturally deprived' changed to 'economically disadvantaged.'

Box 1. Early childhood education in the People's Republic of China

Education within the family

Early childhood education began to receive widespread attention in the eleventh century B.C. in the Chinese West Zhou Dynasty, when a curriculum for young children called 'Six Arts Education' first appeared. In this curriculum, young children were taught to use their right hand as soon as they were able to serve themselves at the table; they were taught to recognize spatial orientations and to read at age 6 and taught courtesy at age 7.

In the seventh century B.C., it was said in *Zuo Zhuan* that young children should be taught to know justice instead of material benefits. In the second

---

century B.C. West Han Dynasty, sayings like this one appeared in the ancient book on education, *Da Dai Li Ji*. *Bao Fu*: "To teach a child while he has no question to ask will make him easier to be trained". Gradually in this dynasty, theories of education began to take shape as it was realized that environment and education had influence in shaping and altering children's knowledge, abilities, and moral character. Later in the second century, *Yan's Family Instructions* indicated clearly that young children cannot be loved without education; otherwise, when the child is grown, the parents will have no prestige, even if they punish the child severely; their anger at his misbehaviour can only arouse his resentment.

The appearance of young children's educational institutions

The first half of the twentieth century saw the establishment of educational institutions for young children and further gradual development of early childhood education in China. This development was due in large part to the contributions made by Tao Xingzhi and Chen Heqin, two Chinese modern educators.

Tao Xingzhi (1891-1946) regarded early childhood education as the foundation of life. He felt that all the important elements for a person's life, such as habit, inclination, and attitude, were mostly determined before six years of age. Beginning in 1927, Mr Tao founded a number of rural kindergartens to serve the common people; in 1934, he created a workers' kindergarten intended for children of women workers in Shanghai. This was in keeping with his belief that: "It is for workers and peasants that we create kindergartens".

Chen Heqin carried out research on child development, conducting a long-term observation of his own child, beginning in 1920. He subsequently published his two books, *Study on child psychology* and *Familial education*. Based on his series of experiments on aspects of curriculum and equipment, he put forward a 15-point proposal for running a kindergarten. Among the 15 points were these:

- the kindergarten must fit the actual situation of China;
- both kindergarten and family should take responsibility for the child's education;

- the curriculum of a kindergarten should be centred on helping children understand the environment and society;
- the first thing that kindergartens should pay attention to is the children's health.
- kindergartens should be a place for developing children's good habits;
- play and games are the major approach for teaching children in kindergartens.
- teachers should be friends with children;
- teaching should be in small groups, in most cases.

A brief introduction to early childhood education since 1949

A new era of early childhood education began with the founding of the People's Republic of China. In the 1950s, the task of kindergartens became the care and education of young children under the education principle of New Democracy. The purpose of kindergartens was to foster healthy development in children before primary school, as well as to lighten mothers' child-care burdens so that they could take part in political, productive, cultural, and educational activities. In January and June of 1955, respectively, the State Council and the Ministry of Education delivered documents calling for factories, the army, and governmental and academic institutions to run their own kindergartens, according to their needs and resources, and asking the local Boards of Education to help in providing the teachers.

In general, government documents at the time conveyed the following ideas: (1) that education for 3-6-year-olds is the first stage of national education; (2) that different resources and organizations should be mobilized to develop early childhood education, both in urban and in rural areas; (3) that there should be clear requirements concerning the educational aims, daily routine, and curriculum appropriate for children; and (4) that efforts must be made to train kindergarten teachers.

Source: Shi Hui Zhong, 1989.
Adapted from "Young children's care and education in the People's Republic of China" by Shi Hui Zhong. In *How nations serve young children: profiles of child-care and education in 14 countries*, Olmstedt, P.P.; Weikart, D.P., (Eds). Ypsilanti, MI: High/Scope Press, 1989, pp. 241-254.

The case for early childhood education

For many reasons, pre-school education is a particularly appealing intervention. In most countries, education has been the traditional means by which people have improved their prospects for productive and satisfying lives.

Many poor children are handicapped when they enter school because they have not had the chance to develop the skills, habits and attitudes expected of the average child in kindergarten and first grade. This lack of development is manifested in their low scores on tests measuring intellectual or scholastic ability. While poor children may be developmentally advanced in other respects, their lack of preparedness for school can lead to unnecessary (preventable) placement in special education classes, to being held back a grade, to repeated scholastic failure and to dropping out of school at an early age.

This idea of giving poor children a 'head start' took hold with educators and social scientists in the 1960s. As many pilot pre-school child-development programmes were mounted, a limited number of scientific evaluations of these programmes were made. As might be expected, most studies assessed the short-term effects of such programmes; only a handful have been able to examine their effectiveness 10 years or more after the programmes had ended.

The most carefully drawn studies of early childhood education programmes suggest a pattern of cause and effect that stretches from early childhood into the adult years. The weight of the evidence from many studies suggests that:

*   Poor children who attend a high-quality early childhood education programme are better prepared for school intellectually and socially.

*   This better start probably helps them achieve greater success in school. Far fewer poor children who have attended good pre-

school programmes need special remedial education, have to repeat a grade, or experience major behavioural problems.

- Their greater success in school tends to lead to greater success in adolescence and adulthood. Their rates of delinquency, teenage pregnancy, and welfare usage are lower, and their rates of high-school completion and subsequent employment are higher. Thus both their economic performance and their social performance greatly improve.

II. Use of child-care settings:
the challenge and policy

With the worldwide increase in out-of-home care and education of young children, the issues involved in developing and providing such services have become the subject of much debate. Information to guide this debate and to serve as a basis for public-policy formation, though scarce at first, is increasingly available.

To begin with, the United Nations (UNESCO, 1989) has provided and continues to provide statistical information related to early child development from 150 countries. In addition, Robert Myers (1992) in *The twelve who survive* presented a comprehensive summary of policy and research in developing countries. Moncrieff Cochran (1993) and authors from 29 countries, in the *International handbook of child-care policies and programmes*, also supplied information from a wide range of countries, including modern, industrialized states such as Sweden and Italy, as well as struggling Third World countries such as Viet Nam and Zimbabwe. What is notable is that none of these sources examined the use of child-care and education services from the family's perspective. That investigation was the goal of the IEA Pre-primary Project sponsored by the International Association for the Evaluation of Educational Achievement (Olmstedt and Weikart, 1989; Olmstedt and Weikart, 1994; Weikart, 1999).

In the multiphase IEA project, researchers surveyed families in each of 11 countries about their use, or non-use, of the early childhood care/education development services that were available: Belgium, China, Finland, Germany, Hong Kong, Italy, Nigeria, Portugal, Spain, Thailand and the USA.

The aim of the survey was to let families speak – to learn firsthand how parents accommodated family needs and beliefs in the light of the child-care/education services they were offered by the public

24

and private sectors. Such information, because it was obtained in as accurate a manner as possible, should serve as a sound basis for national decision-making. By gathering identical types of data from a wide range of countries – those with comprehensive, well-formed early childhood care/education systems and those with patchwork or non-existent systems, those with large-scale private-sector services and those with predominantly government provision – the IEA study provided a picture of the full range of policy options for any country.

Until now, the field of child-care service has been clouded with extensive statements about what families need or want, and these statements have often been expressed by advocates of various points of view. Usually these statements were not research-based, and even government statistics – narrow as they are – are of little use in validating them. One purpose of the IEA study, then, was to provide reliable information, comparable across countries, that could be used for a careful discussion of the issues.

The context of the IEA Pre-primary Project

Still ongoing in 1999, the IEA Pre-primary Project comes at a good time. In addition to parents' growing need for out-of-home care for their pre-school-aged children, there is growing recognition that the early childhood period establishes the foundation for later adult performance. That high-quality early childhood education can significantly improve the life chances of children in general, and those from poor homes and environments in particular, has been confirmed by such longitudinal studies as the (American) High/Scope Perry Pre-school Project (Schweinhart, Barnes, and Weikart, 1993) and the Turkish Early Enrichment Project (Kagitcibari et al., 1988). While there has been little or no comparable research showing that pre-primary programmes can benefit non-poor children to the same extent, policy-makers as well as parents recognize the importance of adequate support for all children during this crucial period of development. In short, need for child-care and realization of the value of early childhood education converge to generate today's extensive support for the provision of pre-primary programmes.

The IEA Pre-primary Project Findings

From the IEA study, a number of issues concerning all the participating nations have emerged. Findings of interest have been described in the sections that follow.

Workforce participation and utilization of care/education services

One of the principal policy findings from this study was that the trend from parent care to out-of-home (or at least extraparental) care/ education for pre-school-aged children was linked to the movement of women into the formal, paid workforce. In all countries studied, this trend was stronger in urban than in rural areas, as might be expected. Indeed, the only countries recording a majority of children exclusively in home care by parents were China (55 %), Nigeria (65 %) and Thailand (63 %) – all countries where rural populations predominate. No other country reported more than 40 per cent of four-year-olds exclusively under parental care.

Perseverance of the trend

Another principal policy finding was that, for two major reasons, this trend towards extraparental care/education is unlikely to be reversed. First, the majority of parents using extraparental services cited their employment as the reason. Where service usage was approximately 80 per cent or higher, as in Germany, Hong Kong, Italy and Spain, the child's need for education or for social-emotional development was cited.

Second, the one issue that might cause a halt or shift in the trend – parental concern about the quality of extraparental care/education the child receives – did not surface in any country. Indeed, at least 92 per cent of parents in every country reported that they were 'somewhat satisfied' or 'very satisfied' with the services their children were receiving. Furthermore, when asked for specific problems encountered with services, most parents in most countries reported few or none.

There were some exceptions. Hong Kong parents reported a range of concerns, including problems with programme philosophy (20 %), with facilities and equipment (21 %), with other children who attended (13 %) and with cost (18 %). Parents in China reported problems with facilities and equipment (10 %) and with qualifications of staff (9 %). Otherwise, the 10,913 parents using extraparental services were largely uncomplaining. For example, no problem area (including 'sick child not accommodated') merited even 1 per cent mention across all those interviewed.

This lack of parental dissatisfaction does not mean that, from a professional point of view, there is no room for improvement in programme quality or delivery. It also does not mean that, from the regulatory perspective, no health or safety shortcomings can be found. It means that while a few families may experience problems, especially those with special medical or educational needs, the average parent either truly has adequate, problem-free services or does not perceive any inadequacies. This finding may be one reason why advocates for meeting the needs of special sub-populations of young children and their families find it difficult to gain widespread support for their causes.

The number of settings attended

Most children who experienced extraparental care/education each week were served in only one extraparental setting. However, a considerable number of children – ranging from 5 per cent in Nigeria to 41 per cent in Belgium – attended a second setting as well. In two countries, small to moderate numbers of children typically attended third and fourth settings each week (Belgium reported 23 % in a third and 5 % in a fourth setting; Germany reported 8 per cent in a third and 8 % in a fourth setting). Thus, since the principal 'cause' of extraparental care/education is the need for child-care while parents work, the need to resort to more than one setting was reported by significant numbers of families in countries where children's services do not cover the full parental workday. Belgium, Germany, Italy and the USA were and are instances of this phenomenon.

Extent of time in extraparental settings

When children are in extraparental care/education, they spend significant time in such settings. While Hong Kong (17 hours per week), Germany (25 hours) and the USA (28 hours) represented the low end of the scale, more typical were the 35 hours found in Spain, Nigeria and Italy and the 55 hours found in Thailand and China. This time in extraparental care/education settings represents a large proportion of a child's life – in the case of a child in Thailand or China, more than half the child's waking hours during the five or six parental workdays each week. Thus, in many countries, the extraparental settings the child experiences plays a large part in forming the child's physical, intellectual and social-emotional growth. Leaving the conduct of these settings to chance, whim or even unquestioned tradition would seem an unwise course for a nation.

Education, a goal for the home setting

In all countries, parents electing to keep their children at home overwhelmingly cited parent-related reasons for doing so. Primarily, these reasons involved parent goals – for example, the goal of being the child's 'first' teacher or educator. (Education of the child in the service setting was also a reason cited by parents who used extraparental settings.) Noteworthy, however, is the fact that a number of parents who keep their children at home do so because they lack an alternative – services either are unavailable or are unsatisfactory in some way. Lack of an alternative was cited especially in China (where 32 % of 'home-care' mothers gave this reason) and, to a lesser extent in Finland (7 %), Germany (8 %), Italy (9 %), Nigeria (9 %) and the USA (10 %).

Sponsors of out-of-home child-care/education

Across the participating countries, the out-of-home child-care/education services that families use were sponsored primarily by governmental or religious organizations. In Finland, Italy and Portugal, at least 50 per cent of all programmes were under government auspices, whereas religious organizations sponsored the majority (60 %) of programmes in Germany and Hong Kong. In

Belgium, all settings had multiple sponsors, with the government always being one of those sponsors, and religious organizations being another for 41 per cent of settings. Private non-religious organizations also played some role, providing 25 to 28 per cent of programmes in Hong Kong, Nigeria and the USA. In spite of the extensive interest in, and discussions about employer-provided care, only China reported a significant percentage of programmes with such sponsorship (28 %), while Finland, Spain and the USA reported only 2 per cent or less; no other countries reported any employer sponsorship. Clearly, corporate- or workplace-sponsored care, while an interesting alternative, is relatively rare.

These findings on service sponsorship suggest that governments and religious organizations continue to be the primary funders and administrators of early childhood care/education programmes. They are also the likeliest source of funds for the vast early childhood service expansion envisaged in most countries. While private institutions will continue to play their part, it appears unlikely that families will have their service needs met through corporate or workplace sponsorship.

Auxiliary services to children

Few group settings offer families and children comprehensive services such as health care, special education services, social services and transportation. The most offered and best-used service is health care. However, services offered are not necessarily used. Only six countries reported health service usage by more than 50 per cent of those to whom it was actually available. Only Belgium reported health care usage by more than half (57 %) of all children in its full survey sample.

Special education and social services, when provided, were lightly used. Fewer than 8 per cent of children in any country received special education or social services through their early education and care programmes. These findings are in spite of the fact that the usual service providers – governmental or religious agencies – are those likely to promote and encourage auxiliary service usage (as does the national Head Start programme in the USA). Fewer than half of the four-year-olds in any country surveyed were offered transportation to their early-childhood programmes. Among those to whom transportation was offered, usage ranged from 22 per cent in Belgium to 65 per cent in China. However, since the survey found that most children lived within a few minutes of the facility they attended, availability of transportation did not appear to be an issue.

Mothers as principal caregivers

Who takes principal responsibility for children's care? In every participating country, regardless of its stage of economic development, mothers took the most responsibility for young children's care and supervision. Of the four-year-old's 16-hour waking day, the time spent with mother (alone or with father) ranged from 8.4 hours (or 53 % of the day) in Belgium to 11.9 hours (or 74 % of the day) in Germany. This contrasted sharply with the hours that fathers were present (with or without mothers), which ranged from 0.9 hour (or 6 % of the day) in China and Hong Kong to 3.7 hours (23 % of the day) in Belgium and 3.5 hours (22 % of the day) in Thailand. Indeed, no country reported 'father only care' amounting to even an hour a day; father's daily time alone with the child ranged from 0.1 hour (6 minutes) in Hong Kong to 0.9 hour (54 minutes) in China. Child-care, in spite of the rhetoric about equality and role sharing in the Western countries, was still very much the responsibility of mothers in all participating countries, regardless of the various cultures and levels of national development involved.

Non-familial caregivers or teachers

Further investigation of children's daily routines indicated that the time children spent with caregivers/teachers other than their parents or relatives varied greatly from country to country. While Belgium reported children spending 6 hours per day in non-familial care, Germany – also a developed European country – reported only 2.1 hours. This was more than Thailand's 1.0 hour, which was below the USA's 2.8 hours. One of the most interesting facts to come out of the daily routine information was that pre-school-aged children in a few countries were left for extended periods of time by themselves, without direct adult supervision. This occurred in China, where 'alone time' constituted 2.9 hours of the child's day, and in Thailand, where it was 0.8 hour of the child's day. Another fact worth noting is this: while Belgium came closest to having non-familial services (in multiple settings) cover a full workday for parents (6 hours), across all participating countries, the average early childhood service coverage was only a portion of the full workday.

Location of children's services

The majority of children spent most of their waking hours either at home (with their mothers) or at a school or organized care centre. An interesting exception was found in Finland, where children averaged more time in a family day-care home (2.4 hours) than in an organized facility (2.1 hours). Time spent in all other possible settings was minimal. The wide variety of locations hypothesized by this study did exist – parks and playgrounds, family day-care homes, workplace arrangements, neighbours' homes – but to a far lesser extent than a worldwide survey might be expected to uncover. Worthy of special note is the finding that transition times (traveling to and from education/care settings) were not a problem, since the average travel time was no more than 15 minutes in most countries.

Final comments

The IEA Pre-primary Project took on a difficult task – the documentation of care/education service usage in 11 participating countries, based on a household survey of parents who have four-year-olds. The international research team was committed to developing survey instruments that represented the best ideas that were acceptable to all. By working as a team, the 11 national research centres achieved this goal without compromising the quality of information attained. Through teamwork, the problems in data collection were resolved, and the complex work was carried out.

Perhaps the most noteworthy finding of this part of the study was this: although pre-school-aged children in all countries were in extraparental or out-of-home care in significant numbers (in most countries, over 60 % typically experience more than two hours of care each week from someone other than a parent), mothers still provided the greatest share of children's care. While the national patterns of early childhood services differed considerably, mothers and paid non-family adults provided the most supervision, and fathers, the least – everywhere. There appear to be two reasons for the increasing use of child services: mothers are entering the paid workforce in increasing numbers throughout the world, and families are seeking advantages for their children in a world they see as highly competitive.

Some social policy analysts may see the spread of the feminist movement or the economic pressures of industrialized society as the issues behind the worldwide demand for early childhood services. Such views only draw the focus away from children. The very real out-of-home care situation that the world's children face demands our careful attention: *children are right now being raised by young people or adults paid to undertake the task rather than by parents or family members. How qualified are these caregivers and educators? What is the quality of children's social interactions in these settings? Are children having the kinds of early childhood experiences that lead to sound child development? Do children's early childhood settings provide the appropriate framework for the development of good workers and good citizens? Are families better off for having such settings to turn to? Countries need to answer these questions.*

III. Expectations for education: what should children experience?

The popular press – and indeed the professional literature – lead us to believe that what we accomplish and how our accomplishments are judged by others are greatly influenced by both our own expectations and those of others. Thus, determining the expectations of young children's teachers and parents is an important aspect of the next phase of the IEA Pre-primary Project. Working co-operatively, the IEA research centre directors from the following (now) 15 nations developed a questionnaire to determine adult expectations about areas of development for four-year-olds: Belgium, China, Finland, Greece, Hong Kong, Indonesia, Ireland, Italy, Nigeria, Poland, Romania, Slovenia, Spain, Thailand and the USA. This questionnaire was administered to both the 1,800 *centre-based* teachers and the 5,000 parents involved in the study. The hope is that by understanding what teachers and parents across various countries expect regarding children's development – what skills they want children to learn and which persons they hold responsible for teaching these skills – we might add to an understanding of children's developmental differences.

At the outset of the IEA Pre-primary Project (Olmstedt and Weikart, 1989; Olmstedt and Weikart, 1994; Weikart, 1999), there was every reason to expect that analysis of study data about expectations would reveal substantial cross-country differences as well as substantial parent-teacher differences within countries. After all, the 15 countries that would be responding to the study's Expectations questionnaire differed linguistically, geographically, economically and politically – to name a few distinctions. No two countries (except for the USA and Ireland) have the same mother tongue. The countries occupy tropical regions (as do Nigeria and Indonesia), temperate regions (as do Italy and Poland) and even an arctic region (as does Finland). Some of the countries (such as Belgium, Italy, or the USA) have advanced industrial economies, while others have newly developing economies. The political systems include both long-established and recently formed democracies, both stable and struggling governments; they represent a mix of communist, socialist and democratic philosophies. The countries also differ in history, cultural tradition (regarding the role of women, for example), ethnic composition and religion.

In light of this diversity, it came as a surprise when the analyses of the Expectations questionnaire data did not reveal substantial differences across these 15 countries. When parents and teachers in country after country were asked to decide which of eight kinds of skills were important for young children to learn, the anticipated differences between countries were not found. Likewise, when these same parents and teachers were asked to assign teacher and parent roles regarding children's learning, there was little disagreement. Even when these parents and teachers were asked to characterize, or define, the eight skill categories that they had identified as important, there was a surprising amount of agreement in the parent and teacher definitions across countries. This is not to say that the study detected no cross-country or within-country differences, but there was far more agreement than disagreement, as the following summary of the expectations findings reveals.

What should pre-school-aged children learn?

A foreign national working in, or visiting, a country quickly becomes aware of the country's unique customs, laws or regulations, ways of conducting social relationships, and so on. Project researchers assumed that in addition to such obvious cross-country differences, they would find deeply rooted cultural values and traditions that shape teacher and parent attitudes in a unique way from country to country. This would result in detectable divergence across countries in how teachers and parents view the important areas of child development. In organizing the study, the 15 national research centre directors agreed on a list of eight generally accepted areas of child development (corresponding to what eventually became the eight 'skill categories' of the Expectations questionnaire). National field tests revealed that these eight areas covered the basic developmental skills of concern to each national group – no additional areas were suggested as necessary to express the interests or goals of either teachers or parents. Upon analyzing the data on teachers' and parents' expectations, regarding the eight skill categories (rank-ordering the categories as to importance, defining them, assigning responsibility for them), researchers found less variation than expected, with teachers agreeing more closely than parents.

What teachers expect: prioritizing eight areas of child development

One important finding from this study of teacher and parent expectations is that there was general agreement across the participant countries about what were the *most important* and the *least important* of the eight skill categories representing the various areas of child development. Teachers in at least 12 of 15 countries named the following three skill categories among the *most important*:

* *Social skills with peers*
  Child learns to share and co-operate with other children, to respect them and to understand their feelings.

* *Language skills*
  Child learns to express his/her thoughts and feelings verbally in a clear and appropriate manner.

* *Self-sufficiency skills*
  Child learns to be independent and to care for him/herself and his/her belongings in a responsible manner.

Also, teachers in at least 10 out of 15 countries named these three skill categories among the *least important*:

* *Pre-academic skills*
  Child learns basic concepts, improves small-muscle co-ordination and begins to master skills necessary for reading, writing and arithmetic.

35

- *Self-assessment skills*
  Child learns to assess his/her own abilities and behaviours, begins to take pride in his/her accomplishments and develops a sense of self-confidence.

- *Social skills with adults*
  Child learns to listen to, co-operate with and respect adults.

The countries involved in these rankings represented the study's complete range of countries (i.e. western European, eastern European, Asian, African). Of course, while no country's teachers were unanimous in their opinion, the extent of agreement on the part of teachers was striking. There was even greater cross-country agreement on some individual categories, such as **social skills with peers** (which teachers in 14 out of 15 countries placed among the *most important*). And teachers agreed about some of the specific *least important* categories almost as much as they agreed about *most important* categories. For example, those in 11 out of 15 countries ranked **social skills with adults** among the *least important*.

The extent of agreement among the more than 1,800 teachers in 15 countries suggests that there is a certain widely accepted view about what constitutes normal early childhood development. Whether this view translates into widespread uniform practice across countries, however, will be revealed only by information gained from direct observation of settings in a later phase of the IEA study.

It is especially noteworthy that teachers in 10 out of 15 countries ranked **pre-academic skills** among the *least important* developmental areas for pre-school-aged children; only in Nigeria and Thailand did teachers rank this category as *most important*. This finding comes at a time when most countries are giving academic performance in elementary school new emphasis. Moreover, this finding about pre-school teachers' opinions of pre-academic skills comes at a time when education is being recognized as a means to create the intellectual base necessary for successful economic development in the post-industrial global society.

What parents expect: prioritizing eight areas of child development

The 5,000 parents involved in this study showed less cross-country agreement than did teachers in ranking the eight skill categories. However, parents in at least 9 of the 14 relevant countries agreed (as did teachers) that these were *most important* for pre-school-aged children (one country did not participate in collecting parent data):

- Language skills;
- Self-sufficiency skills;
- Social skills with peers.

Also, there was general parental agreement in most countries about the areas of development that were *least important*. That is, parents in at least 10 countries ranked these two skill categories among the *least important*:

- Self-assessment skills;
- Self-expression skills;
- Child learns to express him/herself creatively through arts and crafts, music, dance and/or imaginative play.

Congruence between teacher and parent expectations

There is considerable discussion as to whether children do better in educational settings when parents and teachers hold the same as opposed to different views about what is important for children. One view is that the child can move more easily between home and educational setting, feel more welcome in each, learn more effectively, when the expectations of the teacher and the parent are congruent. The alternate view is that children benefit from adults having differing expectations – that lack of congruence between teacher and parent expectations results in the child having a greater variety of activities, different kinds of adult-child relationships, exposure to more than one concept of responsibility, and so on. To provide a basis for exploring this issue, this study statistically compared teachers' and parents' views about the relative importance of the eight skill categories corresponding to the various areas of child development.

The study found that in 8 of the 14 countries, there was a significant correlation between parents' and teachers' rankings of the skill categories. Among these eight countries, there were examples where teachers' and parents' rankings were nearly identical (as was the case in Finland, Romania and Poland, with coefficients of .90 or higher) or at least in solid agreement (as was the case in Nigeria, Belgium, Italy, the USA and Thailand).

How teachers and parents define the areas of child development

While both teachers and parents seemed to agree across most countries that three types of skills – **social skills with peers**, **language skills** and **self-sufficiency skills** – were the most important for young children to develop, this fact alone does not convince us that teachers and parents are talking about exactly the same priorities. Knowing how each group defines these three categories is also necessary. Thus, in every country but China and Slovenia, both teachers and parents were asked to pick out, from a list of 7 to 11 possible subskills, which they considered to be 'the most important' subskills (i.e. the functional definition) for each category. As had been done with the eight major skill categories, the lists of possible subskills for each category had initially been developed and field tested by the 15 co-operating national research centres.

The principal finding from the subskill-selection data was this: not only did parents and teachers in most countries tend to prioritize the areas of development for children in the same way, but they also tended to agree about how their top-priority areas of development were defined. That is, when teachers and parents in a given country both said, for example, that **social skills with peers** were *most important* for young children to develop, both parents and teachers were thinking primarily about the same specific subskills, or behaviours, in that development area.

This finding – that teachers and parents agreed about the functional definitions of the Expectations questionnaire's eight skill categories – is an important one. It gives confidence that teachers' and parents' responses to the ranking procedure in the Expectations questionnaire are the product of their careful thought and consideration.

What teachers and parents predict about each other's expectations for children

While it may be good to know whether teachers and parents agree about what they expect young children to learn, it may be even better to know whether they *understand* each other's expectations, even if they differ. Thus, one part of the Expectations questionnaire asked *teachers* to predict what *parents* might select as priorities for children's learning, and vice versa. The results were as follows.

Teachers were the more accurate predictors. Their predictions of parent priorities most frequently mentioned four areas: **social skills with peers, language skills, self-sufficiency skills** and **pre-academic skills**. The first three of these categories seem to be natural ones for teachers to name in making predictions since, as has been observed, both teachers and parents in many countries give these areas high priority. But predicting the fourth category – **pre-academic skills** – to be a parent priority was interesting, considering that teachers themselves generally ranked **pre-academic skills** among the *least important* for pre-school-aged children (recall that teachers in only two countries ranked this area highly). Thus, the role of these skills in the early education programme certainly is seen in different ways.

When parents were asked to predict teacher priorities, they made two predictions with fairly high accuracy: **social skills with peers** and **language skills**. Two other less accurate predictions parents somewhat frequently made were **pre-academic skills** and **self-**

expression skills. These latter two predictions of parents were only rarely chosen as priorities by teachers. A further analysis of the data suggested that parents had used their own priorities as a basis for predicting what teachers expected pre-school-aged children to learn. Thus, while in most countries teachers understood what parents expected children to learn, unfortunately parents did not have an equally good understanding of teacher expectations.

How teachers and parents assign responsibility for the areas of child development

After looking at what teachers and parents expected children to learn, how congruent their expectations (including their definitions of those expectations) were and how well they understood each other's expectations, it seemed appropriate to ask who should follow-up on those expectations. In other words, who should take responsibility for helping to develop the various kinds of skills in children?

Considering the findings reported up to this point, it should come as no surprise that there was considerable agreement among parents and teachers when they were asked to select, from the eight skill categories, three that they considered important teacher responsibilities and three that they considered important parental responsibilities. Both teachers and parents felt that *teachers* should focus on social skills with peers (10 countries), language skills (7 countries), and self-expression skills (5 countries). Both teachers and parents felt that *parents* should focus on social skills with adults (9 countries), self-sufficiency skills (9 countries) and language skills (6 countries).

How demographics affect teacher/parent expectations

At the outset of this pre-primary study, project researchers hypothesized that important demographic variables of teachers, such as age, experience with four-year-olds, training/education, would differentiate their expectations about what young children should learn. They thought it might be, for example, that younger teachers with more recent training would have different expectations from older teachers. A finding such as this could lead to better understanding and predicting of patterns, which in turn might lead to effective policy recommendations. However, there were no demographic variables in this study that assisted towards that goal.

Possible factors bringing teacher and parent expectations together

As discovered repeatedly in this study of expectations about what children should learn, teachers in most countries and parents in many countries held essentially the same views. Both parents and teachers gave high priority to children learning to get along with others, learning the language, and learning self-care skills. Indeed, when asked to define what a child actually does to accomplish each of these things, teachers and parents again agreed – having social skills with peers means to initiate friendships and to play co-operatively – and this went for each of the developmental areas. Parent and teacher views were not random, and they tended to be largely the same, both within and across most countries.

There were countries that differed in some ways from the majority – Thailand is a good example. Thailand's teachers considered language skills as one of the *least important* areas of development for four-year-olds, while teachers in most other countries said just the opposite. Also, in direct opposition to most other countries, they gave a *most important* rating to self-expression skills and preacademic skills. In fact, neither the teacher nor the parent rankings of Thailand were similar to those of any other country. Yet Thailand's teacher and parent rankings correlated significantly with each other, and when teachers and parents assigned responsibilities for children's learning, they essentially agreed about who would do what.

On the whole, Thailand might be said to have had one of the more unique expectations profiles, but even this profile included similarities with other countries. So even the differences that emerged in this study were not as great as they might have at first appeared to be. What causes this tendency for the expectations of parents – and of teachers – to be more similar than different across a world that is obviously so diverse? Several factors that would tend to bring teachers and parents together may be at work here.

First, as the physician, the nutritionist and the dentist have discovered, children the world over develop in closely similar ways, given adequate opportunity. Bruer (1997), in a summary of brain development research, commented, "Normal children in almost any environment acquire these capacities at approximately the same age – children in affluent suburbs, children in destitute inner cities, children in rural-pastoral settings – throughout the world". Education and child-care professionals have overlooked, perhaps, that children normally mature in similar physical and intellectual patterns. Piaget and other stage theorists have documented that children develop through a similar series of recognizable steps as they grow and gain experience. Teachers working with four-year-olds over a period of years become aware of their typical capacities. For example, four-year-olds do not play games with complex rules and scorekeeping; they need a stable and predictable setting in order to be able to participate, they are ready to use language to direct themselves and interact with other children, they love to imitate what they see, and so on. Parents observe children of friends and relatives, spend hours with their own child, discuss differences between siblings as they mature, and thus also develop at least a basic idea of how children develop. If parents' and teachers' views of what children need are shaped by their actual experience with children day in day out, no other results than the agreement found in this study are possible.

Second, research-centre directors in this 15-IEA study were impressed with the apparent widespread dissemination of information about children's normal growth and development. Through grass-roots child-care, education and nutrition projects like the 75,000-family Hogares Comunitarios Project serving 730,000 children in Colombia, through caregiver training projects like Finland's training programme for home day-care mothers, through the widespread early childhood health and nutrition projects of UNICEF, sound information about child growth and the needs of children has been widely promulgated (Myers, 1992). Add this information to that adults gain by their daily work with children, and uniform expectations like the ones in this study could certainly develop.

Third, a major force in today's world is the globalization of communication, entertainment and commerce. Although the countries participating in this study cover a wide political and philosophical spectrum, all are engaged in efforts to expand their respective economies through export and all recognize the importance of developing an educated populace to support economic expansion. In most countries, citizens support these efforts of government and industry, seeing them as an opportunity to provide a better life for themselves and their families. Thus, parents and teachers of pre-school-aged children do their part by encouraging the young children in their care to get along with others, to take care of themselves and to use language to better their life chances.

IV. Impact of early education: school performance and productivity

There is fundamental logic behind the belief that providing children with early stimulation and improved opportunities will create better performance later on as they tackle the demands of life. Indeed, many cultures have folk sayings equivalent to, "As the twig is bent, so grows the tree". We wish to have children read and comprehend the written word so they may be independent learners and communicate easily; we wish to have children understand the fundamentals of mathematics so they can navigate the higher-order science and technology important to modern society. Therefore, if we are interested in school performance on academic subjects, and if we are concerned about productivity in society, it makes sense to focus on the goals we desire and to set about the task of teaching children what they need to be and to know to reach these goals. Further, it would seem that the earlier we do this, the better.

But with children, things do not work that way! They do not work that way because the child, an extraordinarily complex organism, matures differentially throughout childhood and adolescence. To be ready for adult life, children need to grow through various stages of physical, mental and emotional development, each characterized by unique needs and tasks that support overall growth. This growth, however, accomplishes a great deal more than preparation for academic performance and adult productivity. It includes physical growth from a weak infant with barely functioning, poorly integrated systems to an independent teenager with skilful and integrated physical abilities. It includes psychological growth from the total dependence of an infant, to the emerging independence of an adolescent, to the full independence of responsible adulthood. It includes development from the infant who integrates sound and visual patterns to the adolescent who can read, create, manage language, compute, relate to others and think logically. Thus, the rationale easily applied to adults – 'teach 'em what they gotta know'

– is not useful when applied to children. It does not take into account that the child (infant through adolescent) is in transition and that different teaching and learning strategies are required at different periods of growth. This chapter looks at one basic issue: how child development blends with opportunity-to-learn to produce a long-lasting impact on education and, eventually, on adult productivity.

A brief history of the search for service quality

Over the past 35 years, high-quality care/educational programmes have struggled to find acceptance as a priority for young children. As part of gaining that acceptance, professionals in the field have recognized **the need to define what is meant by a 'high quality' early childhood programme**. Historically, initial efforts to achieve quality have focused on regulation of the health, safety, and nutrition aspects of programmes. This first step is typical of emerging programmes in all countries. Gradually, however, it becomes clear that health, safety and nutrition standards, while necessary, are not sufficient to ensure high-quality early childhood programme operation and outcomes. Once this is recognized, the search for quality expands to introducing standards for caregiver/teacher qualifications, stipulating the training required for programme staff. This done, the focus gradually shifts to a third step, recognition of the need for comprehensive services for the children and families participating in the programme.

To reach the goal of providing high-quality programmes, however, a fourth step is required. A validated, well-implemented, educational methodology must be employed, usually in the form of a model curriculum. As yet, however, this fourth step is not widely recognized as essential.

Age-appropriate education

While there are many approaches, most child-development theories are based on the idea that growth occurs in specific stages. Piaget defined a set of stages that is widely used: sensorimotor (0 to 2 years), pre-operational (2 to 6 years), concrete operational (7 to 10

45

years), and formal operational (11 years and upwards). Neo-Piagetians, like Donaldson (1978), caution that while useful, Piaget's age-ranges must be considered as very flexible. Children develop and mature at different rates, depending on their inborn nature and the range of opportunities provided in their specific environment. Some three-year-olds, for example, may still be very much sensorimotor learners – they might spin the wheels on a truck just to see them spin, rather than to use them as a way to move the vehicle. A few advanced three-year-olds think and express themselves using the language and logic that characterize concrete operational learners; such children, for example, may teach themselves to read. Using age as a general rather than a strict guideline and looking at how children learn, we can examine key organizing principles for educational programmes and what children learn across developmental stages. *Figure 1* summarizes the two Piagetian stages to be discussed. There are implications for teaching and learning that are specifically determined by children's development at each of these stages.

Language and experience are basic

From birth, direct experience with language profoundly impacts children's learning and social development. Sensorimotor and pre-operational children develop language through a complex process that is both genetic and environmental. Basically, very young children acquire sounds and words to match their expanding experience and their knowledge of the world. They build this understanding and use of language through trial-and-error experiences with people and materials. For example, a child learns what 'hot' means through direct, tactile experiences with hot water, stoves, lighted candles and so forth. The suggestion 'Twist the block, then it will fit in the hole' makes sense only when the child has matched the block and the hole many times through trial and error. Children understand words based on their own experiences, and they in turn use words to convey and reflect their own understanding.

Direct experience of the physical world is essential to children's growth and development. Observation and listening are important, but only as elements of direct physical experience with people,

Figure 1.   Organization principles, birth through age six

	Sensorimotor years age 0 to 2 years	Preoperational years age 2 to 6 years
How children learn	Direct experience, active learning; interaction with adult caregivers	Direct experience, active learning; verbal reflection; making decisions
Key progra element	Interactive play based on child's interest	Plan-do-review; representation: telling, drawing, using invented writing
What children learn	Physical reality; developing trust, autonomy, initiative, empathy	Language; exploring classification, seriation, number, space, time, music movement; developing curiosity, initiative, interests, friendships

materials, events and ideas. While adolescents can wrestle with concepts, theories and hypotheses and with such symbols and signs as pictures, written words and recorded images, these abstractions are not in themselves sufficient for learning.

How children learn

A developmental approach assumes that direct experience and active learning are absolutely essential at all stages of children's growth. This approach contrasts with the tendency in schools and in society at large to gradually substitute passive experiences for active ones and to gradually encourage indirect rather than direct experiences. Children need direct experiences to learn what things really are and what effects they produce. Children do not know how to pour water into a container until they have played with water and various containers over and over again. It will not do simply to tell them, or to offer a visual demonstration, or even to provide a one-time hands-on play opportunity.

For the *sensorimotor* (infant-toddler) child, an essential aspect of direct experience and active learning is ongoing interaction with positive, supportive adult caregivers. Infants and toddlers need eye contact, 'partnered' communication, touching and close body-contact with adults. Realizing this, most adults rock babies; sing lullabies; pat their backs to a steady beat; and bathe, feed, care for and play with them. These interactions with attentive adults are critical to children's learning and social development. How these interactions are accomplished and how often, of course, differs, from culture to culture.

Rapid verbal development distinguishes the *pre-operational* (pre-school) child. In addition to offering children direct experience and active learning, providing support for their verbal reflection and independent decision-making becomes increasingly important. While children communicate and follow their interests from birth onward, the opportunity for reflecting on their experiences in their own words and making their own decisions are additional ingredients for pre-operational growth and development. For example, when a child engages in a conversation about a topic of personal interest and an attentive adult listens, comments, and asks a related open-ended question, the child has the opportunity to think aloud, decide the direction and content of the conversation, and experience adult respect and partnership.

A key programme element: plan-do-review

During the *sensorimotor period*, infants and toddlers need to play to develop a sense of independence and to explore things that attract their attention. However, simply having a rich environment with ample opportunity to explore is not sufficient. Children also need to interact in two-way communication with positive, supportive adults. For example, by taking turns with Steven, observing and following his interests and initiatives, and allowing him to control the pace of events, adults support, use language and respond to the child's needs. Steven, in turn, develops a sense of trust and initiative.

During the *pre-operational period*, the plan-do-review sequence supports actions initiated by the pre-schooler. Adults encourage children to plan – to express their intentions – by asking, for example, 'What do you think you will do with all those blocks?' Children then carry out their intentions, or plans; and this *do* stage may last a few minutes or more than an hour. Dramatic play involving several children, 'cooking' to 'feed' fellow playmates, or creating shell structures and patterns are the types of things that occur during the *do* stage. After each work period, adults encourage children to *review* their experiences. The children may talk about what they did or express themselves in drawing or in 'writing'. In so doing, children begin to exercise memory skills and develop insight about their experiences.

What children learn

As *sensorimotor* infants and toddlers explore their worlds, they are learning about physical reality. Since everything they encounter is brand-new to them, they have to discover things for themselves by tasting, chewing, smelling, pushing, pulling, banging, throwing,

49

holding, hearing and seeing. When they explore the physical world with the full support of caregivers who play with and care for them as partners, infants and toddlers also begin to relate to people in a way that allows them to form a positive, hopeful view of themselves and trustful relationships with others.

The *pre-operational* (pre-school) child is involved in matching language to actions and finding out about the physical world from a more logical perspective, with a focus on relationships in the areas of classification, seriation, number, space and time. The child can use materials, toys and tools; work next to and in partnership with others; and relish the joy of trying things out and making them work through trial and error. Out of these active experiences come dispositions to be curious, to initiate relationships with others and to enjoy exploring and learning. Strangely, it is not only the actual knowledge of logical relationships gained during this period, but also the manner in which children interact with people, materials, events and ideas to gain this knowledge, that is critical to pre-operational learning and its lifelong consequences.

Of these two stages – sensorimotor (infant-toddler) and pre-operational (pre-school) – which is more important? Is there any intervention at these stages that has any value later, especially for educational performance and adult productivity? The next section of this chapter examines the information on these two issues for each of the age groups.

Infant-toddler programmes: evidence of effectiveness (birth to age two)

With the growing awareness of the long-term impact of high-quality pre-school programmes, some suggest that if intervention could be provided from birth, problems of developmental lag and inadequate growth could be avoided. If pre-school education is effective at ages two to six, programmes from birth to age two would make success even more possible. However, long-term effectiveness of infant-toddler educational programmes has not yet been satisfactorily demonstrated. So far, little or no evidence is available to support the hypothesis that intervention from birth to age two will alone improve the educational performance and social growth of the child in later years. The available evidence indicates a limited contemporary effect from the best programmes but no results lasting even a year later, let alone extending into primary school and adulthood. Typical infant-toddler programmes fail to find even that much effect. This is not to say that this stage is not important and that normal development cannot go awry. *It is to say that what will produce normal skill development between birth and age two has so far seemed to be available to most children. It is important to note, however, that programmes ensuring health, nutrition, immunization, attachment to a caring adult and related issues are very effective in increasing infant physical growth and well-being.*

Perhaps one of the most carefully controlled studies, and one of the earliest, was the High/Scope-Carnegie Infant Education Project (Lambie et al., 1974). Initiated in the autumn of 1967, this project enrolled 88 infants and their mothers from disadvantaged families in Ypsilanti, Michigan, USA. The infant-mother pairs were assigned at random to one of three conditions: a treatment group that received weekly home visits by staff professionals, a contrast group that received weekly home visits by community volunteers and a control group that received no services. Infants entered the programme at either 3, 7, or 11 months of age and participated for 16 months. This design permitted the study of both the type of treatment and the age of entry. Of the 88 children enrolled, 65 completed the full 16-month project.

The project had a comprehensive research design, and the progress of both mothers and infants was carefully followed. The findings at the end of the project were most encouraging: "Over all test points ... there were significant programme effects: infants in the experimental group scored significantly higher language and intelligence measures on the average than children in either the contrast or control groups." However, "One year after the programme terminated, the treatment group differences on the Stanford-Binet Intelligence Scale did not reach ... statistical significance" (Lambie et al., 1974, p. 116). Since this project was designed as a longitudinal study, the children and their mothers were followed up again when the children were in second grade (age 7). As found in this follow-up, "Significant group differences ... favouring the experimental treatment group at the end of the programme were no longer present five years later" (Epstein and Weikart, 1979, p. 41). The findings of this project, unfortunately, are reflected in the findings concerning most work with parents and infants to date.

As the High/Scope-Carnegie Infant Education Project was exploring new ground in providing educational service to infants and their mothers, later efforts were perhaps more effective. Major efforts have been mounted under a variety of auspices. Most notable was the multi-year, multi-project Ford Foundation Child Survival/ Fair Start Project (Larner et al., 1992). This project was a multi-site undertaking with teams of local practitioners and researchers in seven diverse communities developing and implementing preventive programmes for parents and their infants. The primary goal was "... a preventive focus on pregnancy and infancy, offering education, support (to families), and information about appropriate services" (p. 7). The programmes spanned ages 10 months to 22 years. Reflecting the surprising lack of findings for such a major programme with outstanding staff talent and funding resources, the research team of High/Scope evaluators contracted by the Ford Foundation summarized the study outcomes under the heading 'Modest Outcomes'. They said, "Clearly there are limits to the benefits we can expect to see from participation in comparatively modest, multi-purpose programmes like the CS/FS programmes" (p. 245). What 'modest' findings there were occurred in the health-care and parent-education areas, not in child development.

A general review of all such studies was published by the Centre for the Future of Children. St. Pierre, Layzer and Barn (1995) summarized six large-scale research programmes at 500 sites with parents and infants, including those programmes that went on to include pre-school services. The review looked at all the major projects of the 1980s and 1990s. These programmes provided comprehensive services, including parent education and literacy training, with support to the children. All were evaluated.

These projects operated without the usual limitations of funds; some programmes cost as much as $13,000 to $16,000 per family, whereas the more typical programme costs were in the $2,000 to $4,000 range. Nevertheless, the overall results were limited. St. Pierre et al. (1995) summarized the findings tersely: "Evidence about the short-term effects of two-generation programmes is mixed ... As currently designed, two-generation programmes have small short-term effects on a wide set of measures of child development" (p. 89). These are hardly results that social planners and policy-makers can use to justify the expenditure of limited funds on such efforts. And "small, short-term effects" rarely precede greater differences at a later time.

The possibility of gaining improved educational performance and better productivity through programmes for infants and toddlers would appear limited. While new programme delivery methods and new insights gained from basic research into physical development may open new avenues, the current approaches appear exhausted. Again, it should be noted that there is success at this age in delivering health, nutrition and other basic needs services. The apparent uniform, limited findings on educational and social development gains to date should in no way interrupt these other basic programmes. The findings on pre-school programmes are in sharp contrast to those on infants and toddlers. Pre-school findings are presented next.

Pre-school programmes: evidence of effectiveness (ages two to six)

Examination of the literature reveals that evidence for the effectiveness of high-quality pre-school programmes for children living in poverty comes from a range of sources. The Head Start Synthesis Project meta-analysis of all available studies of Head Start's effects (McKey et al., 1985) identified 50 studies that found evidence of immediate improvements in children's intellectual performance, socio-emotional performance, and health, and these lasted several years. It also found that these Head Start programmes provided and linked families with health, social, and educational services and influenced various institutions to provide such services. Ramey,

Bryant and Suarez (1985) identified another 11 experimental studies in which the mean intelligence test scores of children who participated in pre-school programmes were as high as, or higher than, the mean intelligence test scores of children in the studies' control groups. Lazar, Darlington, Murray, Royce and Snipper (1982) analyzed data from the constituent studies of a collaborative effort called the Consortium for Longitudinal Studies. They reported findings of positive programme effects on intelligence test scores at school entry, on special education placement, and on grade retention. Barnett (1995) presented the most recent survey of the most relevant studies. Finally, Myers (1995) summarized studies on all aspects of early childhood development research from throughout the world and reports evidence of "the importance of promoting healthy development during the early years" (p. 435).

Fade-out of pre-school programme effects

Although some have claimed that most effects of good pre-school programmes for children in poverty fade away (e.g. McKey et al., 1985), there is virtually no evidence of fade-out of the effect on children's special education placement, high school graduation or delinquency. Fade-out evidence is mixed for effects on children's socio-emotional behaviour and school achievement. Clear evidence of fade-out has been found only for gains in children's intelligence-test scores. In the 1960s, the hypothesis was that though early educational programmes were found to raise young children's test scores, subsequent educational programmes would not affect them. Instead, it may be argued that a difference in intelligence-test scores reflects a difference in educational settings. When children who have attended pre-school programmes and children who have *not* attended pre-school programmes come together into the same standard elementary-school classrooms, their intelligence-test scores also come together.

The High/Scope Perry Pre-school study

By virtue of its careful experimental design and long-term duration, the evaluation of the High/Scope Perry Pre-school programme is one of the most thorough examinations of programme effects ever undertaken (Schweinhart, Barnes and Weikart, 1993). The basic research question was whether the High/Scope Perry Pre-school programme affected the lives of participating children. The study focused on 123 African-Americans born in poverty and at high risk of failing in school. In the early 1960s, at ages three and four, these children were randomly divided into a programme group that received a high-quality, active-learning pre-school programme (the High/Scope Curriculum) and a group that received no pre-school programme. The two groups were carefully studied over the years. Researchers interviewed 95 per cent of the original study participants at age 27 and also gathered data from their school, social services and public records. Assuming that post-pre-school differences between the groups represent pre-school programme effects, the following findings about pre-school programme effects were statistically significant (with a two-tailed probability of less than .05):

- *Social responsibility*: By age 27, only one-fifth as many programme group members as non-programme group members were arrested five or more times (7 % v. 35 %), and only one-third as many were ever arrested for drug dealing (7 % v. 25 %).

- *Earnings and economic status*: At age 27, four times as many programme group members as non-programme group members earned $2,000 or more per month (29 % v. 7 %). Almost three times as many programme group members as non-programme group members owned their own homes (36 % v. 13 %), and over twice as many owned second cars (30 % v. 13 %). Significantly fewer programme group members than non-programme group members received welfare assistance or other social services at some time as adults (59 % v. 80 %).

- *Educational performance*: One-third again as many programme group members as no-programme group members graduated from regular or adult high school or received General Education Development certification (71 % v. 54 %). Earlier in the study, the programme group had significantly higher average achievement scores (at age 14) and literacy scores (at age 19) than the non-programme group.

• **Commitment to marriage**: Although the same percentages of programme males and non-programme males were married (26 %), the programme males were married nearly twice as long as the non-programme males (an average of 6.2 years v. 3.3 years). Five times as many programme females as non-programme females were married at the time of the age-27 interview (40 % v. 8 %). Programme females had only about two-thirds as many out-of-wedlock births as did non-programme females (57 % of births v. 83 % of births).

• **Return on investment**: A benefit-cost analysis was conducted by estimating the monetary value of the programme and its effects in constant 1992 dollars discounted annually at 3 per cent. Dividing the $88,433 in benefits per participant by the $12,356 in cost per participant, results in a benefit-cost ratio of $7.16 returned to the public for every dollar invested in the High/Scope Perry Pre-school programme. The programme was an extremely good economic investment, better than most other public and private uses of society's resources. By increasing the number of children per adult from five to eight, the programme's cost per child per year could be reduced, with virtually no loss in quality or benefits.

Early childhood education, when offered as a high-quality programme, is a powerful antidote to poverty. Such programmes are obviously not the only solution. For example, not all children who attended the Perry Pre-school programme benefited or graduated from high school and, as adults, 71 per cent earned less than $2,000 a month. Yet, programme participation did improve the life chances of participants and did significantly reduce the pool of those needing additional help or creating major social problems for the community.

Since educational programmes at ages two to six (the pre-operational level of development) have proved to be effective, the question now is this: Is intervention at pre-school age all that is needed, and does it matter which educational approach is used? The next chapter considers this question.

Figure 2.   Pre-school curriculum models

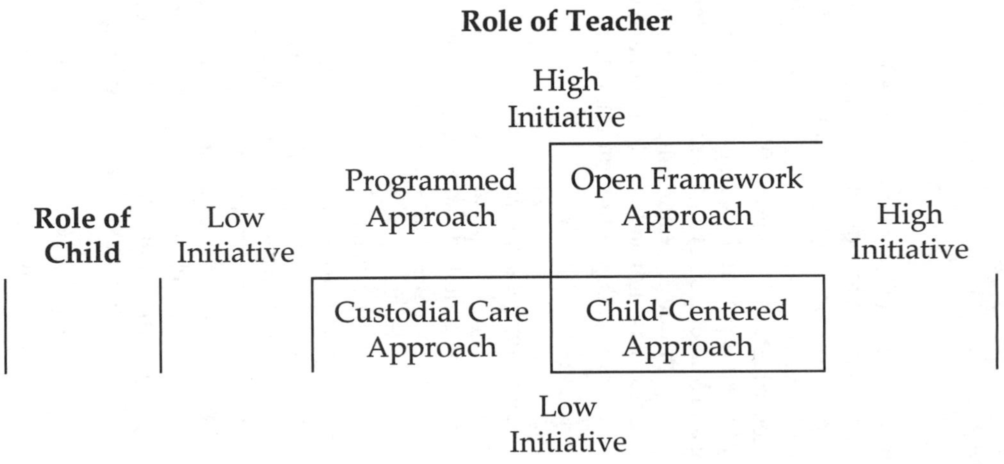

Role of Teacher

	High Initiative	High Initiative
Role of Child Low Initiative	Programmed Approach	Open Framework Approach
	Custodial Care Approach	Child-Centered Approach
		Low Initiative

V. Early childhood education curriculum models: does every programme work?

The various educational approaches used with children generally fall into four different categories, as shown in *Figure 2*. Use of these categories permits curriculum-model description and research to proceed with greater efficiency. While this categorization pattern was first described by Weikart (1972), other observers have used essentially the same pattern for categorizing early childhood curricula (Kohlberg and Mayer, 1972) and parenting styles (Baumrind, 1971). The organizing principle behind this pattern is that in a learning situation, the teacher/adult and the child can each take a role of either high or low initiation, depending on the intention of the curriculum theory employed.

In the ***programmed approach***, which includes methods drawn from learning theory, the typical role of the teacher is to determine and then initiate the required learning activities; the role of the child is to respond and to learn from what the teacher offers, not to self-initiate individual learning or activities. These curricula include clearly defined objectives; incorporate carefully designed, programmed sequences to move children towards these objectives; and provide teachers with a script, or explicit instructions, for implementing the sequences. Content usually emphasizes specific pre-academic skills. Learning is viewed as the acquisition of 'correct' responses with respect to the programmed-instruction goals. It is assumed that if the behavioural objectives are specific enough, virtually anything can be taught to almost any child through the use of appropriate behaviour-modification techniques.

In the ***open-framework approach***, which is based on development theory, it is the role of both teacher and child to initiate learning activities. The primary educational objective for the child is the development of fundamental cognitive processes and concepts, rather than specific skills (although it is assumed that specific skills

58

will be acquired during general development). Learning results from the child's intended, direct experience in and action upon the environment, followed by shared reflection on the experience. Learning is not viewed as an accumulation of specific pieces of information, as in the programmed learning approach. Open-framework curricula are generally based on an explicit theory of child development (e.g. the High/Scope Curriculum draws on Piagetian theory). This theory provides a decision-making framework for teachers without specifying the day-to-day content of the programmes. Children identify the content and interests that are of most importance to them, and learning occurs through the child's active and largely intrinsically motivated involvement in an environment structured and observed by the teacher.

In the ***child-centred approach***, which is based on social development and maturation theories, the child typically initiates learning by playing, and the teacher's role is to respond to the child's particular interests and activities. The great majority of pre-school programmes around the world would describe themselves as being in this category. Characterized by a focus on the development of the 'whole child', such programmes emphasize social and emotional growth and self-expression, rather than acquisition of specific pre-academic skills or cognitive development. Classroom environments are typically open and, ideally, rich in stimuli. The relationship between teacher and child tends to be permissive. Content revolves around topics of interest to the child that support general socialization-enculturation, opportunities for children's independent and creative activities and opportunities for children's exploration and development of healthy peer relationships.

The ***custodial approach*** has the teacher/adult providing basic care while the children entertain themselves. In some cases – in programmes that focus on specific health and nutrition goals – the children remain passive in cribs or certain sections of the room, waiting for the next event, such as toileting or snack time. Unless called for by schedule, there is little interaction between caregiver and children. Often there is little activity undertaken by children. (This approach is adopted in some programmes in developing countries. In fact, some UNICEF-supported *and other health or nutrition aid* programmes that view themselves as 'child-centred' *often* fall into this category). However, it has no basis in theory and is not recommended.

The next section looks at the research undertaken to examine the differential impact of these approaches. Carrying out such programme-comparison research is more difficult than implementing research on a single programme, because equality in the programmes must be maintained and random assignment of participants is essential. Few studies are able to meet these criteria.

Studies comparing pre-school curricula

Three long-term studies

Three long-term pre-school curriculum comparison studies begun in the 1960s focused on children living in poverty and included Direct Instruction (the programmed approach), the High/Scope Curriculum (or another open-framework approach), and traditional Nursery School programmes (the child-centred approach). The studies are the High/Scope Pre-school Curriculum Comparison study (Schweinhart and Weikart, 1997), the University of Louisville study of Head Start (Miller and Bizzell, 1983), and the University of Illinois study (Karnes et al., 1983). All three studies collected data using a variety of measures of intellectual performance, as well as data from interviews and records. All three studies found that on various measures of intellectual performance, children in Direct Instruction programmes initially outperformed children in child-centred and other kinds of programmes. But these significant differences appeared only during the programme and up to a year afterward. In other words, the widely observed pattern of IQ improvement followed by fade-out applied to the pre-school programmes involved in these three long-term studies. In the Illinois study, the high-school graduation rates of study participants were noticeably, if not significantly, different across programme types – 70 per cent for the child-centred programme group, 48 per cent for the Direct Instruction programme group, and 47 per cent for the study's no-programme group. However, among these three studies, only the High/Scope Pre-school Curriculum Comparison study met the criteria for random assignment of sample.

The Planned Variation Head Start Study

In the late 1960s, national Head Start began a long-term study to examine the effects of using different pre-school curriculum models. This 1969-72 Planned Variation Head Start project included a dozen different pre-school curriculum models at 37 sites with some 6,000 children enrolled in the model programmes (Datta et al., 1976). Among the dozen models studied were the Direct Instruction model (programmed approach); the High/Scope model (open-framework approach); and an 'Enabler model', which resembled a traditional child-centred approach. Although study participants were children enrolled in Head Start, they were nevertheless heterogeneous in family socio-economic status and initial intellectual performance. Despite the study's many design problems, two clear findings emerged. First, on the post-programme *achievement tests*, children in Direct Instruction and other programmed-learning programmes had higher scores than did children in any of the other programmes or in any of the comparison groups. Second, *in intellectual performance*, children in High/Scope programmes had greater gains than children in all other models. High/Scope programme children gained an average of 23 points on the Stanford-Binet Intelligence Scale, while children in all other models gained no more than five points.

Recent short-term pre-school studies

A number of other early childhood curriculum comparison studies have been conducted in the USA and in Portugal. For example, Burts, Charlesworth, Hart and their associates have engaged in a programme of research based on assessing teachers' developmentally appropriate beliefs and practices (as defined by the National Association for the Education of Young Children) (Bredekamp, 1987) and related child outcomes. 'Developmentally appropriate practice' corresponds to the High/Scope and child-centred models, while 'developmentally inappropriate practice' corresponds in many ways to the Direct Instruction model. Examining a sample of 37 kindergarten children, they found that those in a developmentally inappropriate class exhibited significantly more stress behaviours (such as complaints of feeling sick, stuttering, fights, tremors, nervous laughter and nail biting) than did those in a developmentally appropriate class (Burts et al., 1990). They replicated this finding with a sample of 204 kindergarten children and found these curriculum group differences to be most pronounced for males and for African-American children, the categories of children most likely to experience Direct Instruction classes (Burts et al., 1992).

In other curriculum comparison research, DeVries and her associates systematically observed three kindergarten classes – one used Direct Instruction, another used an open-framework approach like High/Scope's and the third used an eclectic approach. Analyzing teachers' interactions with children, they found that the open-framework teacher significantly surpassed the other two in her use of reciprocal and collaborative negotiation strategies and shared experiences (DeVries et al., 1991). Analyzing children's interactions with one another during two game-like activities, they found that compared with children in the Direct Instruction and eclectic programmes, children in the open-framework programme were more interpersonally interactive and had a greater number and variety of negotiation strategies and shared experiences (DeVries et al., 1991). Although *before* kindergarten and in first grade the Direct Instruction class had significantly higher achievement-test scores than did the open-framework class, these significant differences between the two classes disappeared by third grade.

Comparative curriculum research is important to the extent that the curriculum models compared represent the real choices made by early childhood teachers. Marcon (1992, 1994) identified these three different pre-school models actually used by teachers and operating in the Washington, D.C. public schools: teacher-directed, child-initiated and 'middle-of-the-road'. Marcon's research examined the development of a random sample of 295 children attending these three types of programmes. The teacher-directed programmes resembled Direct Instruction, and the child-initiated programmes resembled High/Scope. Children from the various types of classes differed significantly in their mastery of basic reading, language and mathematics skills, with the greatest mastery being shown by children from child-initiated classes, followed by children from teacher-directed classes, then by children from 'middle-of-the-road' classes. Although not statistically significant, this same differential ranking by curriculum type appeared later, in fourth grade, in children's grade-point averages overall and in most subject areas.

Other curriculum comparison findings came from the High/Scope Training of Trainers Evaluation (Epstein, 1993). In this evaluation, Epstein found that compared with children in nominated high-quality classes not using the High/Scope Curriculum, children in High/Scope classes were rated significantly higher at the end of the school year in their initiative, social relations, music and movement skills, and general development. In another study of the effects of the High/Scope Curriculum, Frede and Barnett (1992) found that pre-school programmes throughout South Carolina that were implementing the High/Scope Curriculum moderately to very well, contributed more to children's school achievement at kindergarten and first-grade entry than did programmes with low implementation levels. With these general findings as a base, the next section looks at a long-term study specifically designed to investigate the question of model effectiveness in reaching improved education and adult productivity goals.

The High/Scope Pre-school Curriculum Comparison Study

The High/Scope Pre-school Curriculum Comparison Study began in 1967 (Schweinhart and Weikart, 1997). The project employed a stratified random-assignment procedure to assign 68 disadvantaged three- and four-year-old children (both African-American and Anglo) living in Ypsilanti, Michigan, to each of three curriculum models: Direct Instruction (programmed approach), High/Scope (open-framework approach) and traditional Nursery School (child-centred approach). The children attended school for one or two years. Children in each group attended a daily 22-hour classroom session and received a home visit to involve their parents for 90 minutes every other week. The findings on curriculum group differences through age 23 concerning education, household and life adjustment (particularly the number of criminal arrests) are summarized here. Comparisons can be drawn between these findings and those of the High/Scope Perry Pre-school Study.

Education. Only one significant group difference in total education-related scores took place during the study through to the age of 23: the Direct Instruction group surpassed the traditional Nursery School group at the end of the pre-school programme, at age five, on the Stanford-Binet Intelligence Scale. The larger finding from tests is the extraordinary increase in the mean IQ of the whole sample of children, whatever curriculum model they experienced. From the baseline mean IQ of 78 at age three, the three curriculum groups together at age four, after one year of a pre-school programme, evidenced an improvement of 26 points. This improvement diminished by nine points during the subsequent six years, but held steady at 17 points above the baseline at ages six, seven and ten, which is a pattern of sustained improvement that contradicted the expected IQ fade-out.

However, despite the Direct Instruction group's two years of intensive academic preparation, all three curriculum groups performed essentially the same on academic tests throughout their school years. The Direct Instruction group experienced significantly more years of special education for emotional impairment or disturbance; members of the other two groups experienced almost no special education. Members of the Direct Instruction group failed almost twice as many classes as did members of the other two curriculum groups, a difference that was not statistically significant but that was consistent with the Direct Instruction group's non-significant pattern of a lower rate of on-time high school graduation.

Household. Age 23 is the very beginning of adult life and is still very much a transitional period. The striking evidence of this is that nearly half of the follow-up study's respondents (47 %) were, at age 23, living with their mother and/or father, that is to say, living in their home of origin. Curriculum groups differed significantly in the percentages of members married and living with their spouses: 0 per cent of the Direct Instruction group, as compared with 18 per cent of the Nursery School group and 31 percent of the High/Scope group. This finding resembles the High/Scope Perry Pre-school study finding that 40 per cent of programme females, but only 8 per cent of non-programme females, were married at age 27 (N = 49).

Life adjustment (*criminal arrests*). The Direct Instruction group experienced over twice as many *lifetime arrests*, including twice as many adult arrests, as either of the other two curriculum groups. The Direct Instruction group averaged 3.2 lifetime arrests per person, as compared with 1.5 for the High/Scope group and 1.3 for the Nursery School group.

Most important, the Direct Instruction group had significantly more felony arrests than the other curriculum groups – four times as many as the other groups combined. These differences appeared in felony arrests from ages 22 to 25, as the number of these arrests grew more substantial. Forty-three per cent of Direct Instruction group members had felony arrest records, as compared with only 10 per cent of the High/Scope group and 17 per cent of the Nursery School group.

Compared with the High/Scope group, the Direct Instruction group also identified significantly more *sources of irritation* in the community (the interview item asked the respondent to identify 'different types of people ... giving you a hard time lately'). The most frequent sources of irritation identified were collection agencies, work supervisors, police, courts and family members. The prominence of police and courts, particularly for the Direct Instruction group members, corroborates the findings of differences in numbers of felony arrests.

Finally, the Direct Instruction group reported being *suspended from work* significantly more often than did either of the other two curriculum groups – 0.6 times per group member as compared with almost no work suspensions in the other groups.

Curriculum models and programme quality

This study suggests that using specific curriculum models that support children's initiative is essential to having high-quality pre-school programmes that produce lasting benefits. In particular, it suggests that education officials who promote teacher-scripted instruction with young children living in poverty are pursuing a very risky path. Programmes and teachers who want the effects that are found to result from a particular curriculum model must commit to following the curriculum model. Research findings regarding programme effects can be generalized only to programmes that are essentially the same as the programmes studied. Similar research by Nabuco and Sylva (1995) support the idea that curriculum may be more important than culture, socio-economic or racial factors. But following a curriculum model does not require abandoning intelligent judgement, as some scholars have suggested (Goffin, 1993; Walsh et al., 1993). Situations in pre-school programmes are constantly changing; teachers must apply principles intelligently to these situations, or the principles are reduced to mindless reactions. On the other hand, while this study suggests that conventional early childhood wisdom is on the right track, it hardly substantiates every idea that a good early childhood educator ever had.

For one thing, this study should dispel any belief that home visits and teacher-parent contacts alone make the difference between programmes that have lasting beneficial effects and those that do not. Bi-weekly home visits were as much a part of the Direct Instruction programme as they were of the others. Nevertheless, this study does leave open the question of whether substantial outreach to parents is one of the aspects of a curriculum model that can reinforce its lasting benefits. Had the parents not been full partners in the implementation of the child-centred and open-framework curriculum models with their children, perhaps these curriculum groups would not have differed significantly from the Direct Instruction group in their average number of felony arrests at age 23.

This High/Scope Pre-school Curriculum Comparison Study supports advocacy of open-framework education over teacher-scripted instruction for young children. It identifies the High/Scope Curriculum and to some extent the traditional Nursery School approach as particular methods of education that develop in children the decision-making capacity and social skills needed for responsible adult life. It indicates that these approaches might help prevent crime. *It shows that choice of a curriculum model is an important factor in determining the quality of early childhood education.*

Lessons for public policy

The lessons for public policy are straightforward. Children aged two to six years old who participate in high-quality, active learning programmes in any context (family, home care, centre-based) where they have the opportunity to choose and plan activities and independently develop their choices will be better students in school and more productive citizens as they mature. Teaching children of this age didactically, no matter how logical it is to adult planners and administrators, is counter-productive. While there is little high-quality research to support the claim, there is every reason to believe that this public-policy lesson is valid for most rural-urban children in most cultural and linguistic groups around the world. Investment in educational programmes for children from birth to age 22 has not yet been shown to be advantageous, although programmes at that age range can be effective as delivery systems for health, nutrition and various family support requirements.

Figure 3.   Criteria for selecting a curriculum model

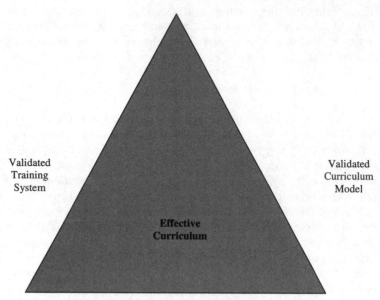

Validated
Training
System

Validated
Curriculum
Model

**Effective
Curriculum**

Validated Assessment System
Child Progress/Programme Implementation

VI. An effective curriculum model: selection and use

The admonishment provided by the cluster of studies examining the issue of effective approaches to early childhood care and education is very specific: *use those curriculum models that are based on child-initiated learning supported by adults, rather than ones that consist of adult-structured lessons. While this finding is a little surprising, it is fortunate, because it supports a desirable public-policy goal: to engage professionals, families and communities in the care and education of children in ways that allow each group to implement their own ideas and objectives.* A curriculum model that emphasizes child-initiated learning best promotes this type of engagement because it is *focused on process rather than content.* Because it is not scripted, and therefore not closely determined by a government agency or by a textbook publisher, a curriculum incorporating child-initiated learning allows for including local traditions, games, songs, stories and found materials. Adults with knowledge of the local community can support and extend children's interests in these familiar objects and activities. This openness permits recognition of the wide differences among children within a given classroom or centre.

While an open-framework approach with an emphasis on child initiation and active adult support is important, there are even broader criteria for selecting a curriculum model that will lead to the desired results; these are indicated in *Figure 3*. To be effective, a high-quality pre-school model needs to meet three requirements: (1) it must have a validated curriculum; (2) it must have a validated training system; and (3) it must have a validated assessment system.

A validated curriculum

To be effective, a curriculum model must be based on developmentally valid theory or beliefs. Its carefully thought-through organizing principles need to form a logical system, which then becomes the basis for making decisions about day-to-day programme operation and practice (setting up the learning environment, daily routine, adult-child interaction, logistics of teacher planning, nature and extent of parent involvement, organization of learning activities, resolution of conflicts, use of technology). In the High/Scope pre-school model, Piaget's ideas about understanding the child's development of knowledge, and Dewey's ideas about the importance of participatory learning at all age levels, serve as the organizing principles.

The theoretical basis of a model provides a discipline for both programme developers and adults who apply the approach. If the teacher or caregiver can elect to introduce into the pre-school programme anything that is of passing interest, or if the programme is simply an amalgamation of several ideas that might be described as 'good practices', then there is the danger of becoming eclectic. An eclectic programme lacks coherence and does not lend itself to documentation, replication and, finally, validation. While a given eclectic curriculum may be very successful, it is essentially one of a kind and, because it cannot be replicated or validated, is of little use in planning community- or nationwide early childhood services.

A pre-school model must be able to be documented if it is to be understood and used by a wide range of individuals from different educational and social backgrounds. While it is always difficult to document a programme, to write down its features and practices, such a step is essential in making the programme accessible to others. The process of documentation also forces the developers to clarify the programme's goals and methods. Once written down, it can be adapted for adults with limited skills, so community members and other paraprofessionals can participate in programme operation. It forms the basic body of knowledge for training new staff and explaining the programme to parents and other interested parties. It is available for translation into the language of any country where the approach would be useful. It can be extended for use by others working with different groups, such as children with special educational needs or multilingual children. For the High/Scope approach, the textbook Educating young children (Hohmann and Weikart, 1995) is the most recent documentation. There are many other supporting print and recorded materials developed to help adapt the content of Educating young children to specific groups of adults and of children. Many of these materials are now available not only in English, but also in Arabic, Turkish, Dutch, Portuguese, Spanish, Finnish, Chinese, French, Norwegian and Korean.

A model system needs to be validated by research demonstrating significant effects when the model is well implemented. This absolute requirement for validation of long-term effectiveness is the one that most model approaches fail to meet. So often in education, especially with programmes for young children, adults use ideas that they like. They are pronounced as valid practice because of direct and immediate experience. Yet, as seen in early chapters, practices that seem logical and built upon tradition or applied in different contexts often do not work to produce desired outcomes. Only well-designed, longitudinal studies can provide answers to permit the expenditure of public funds on a wide scale. Such studies are neither cheap nor quick. They are very difficult to design, fund and carry out. But they are essential to justify the wide-scale use of specific models to solve social and educational problems. For the High/Scope approach, the long-term High/Scope Perry Pre-school study offers significant validation of the model's impact throughout childhood and into adulthood. This groundbreaking study receives support from the High/Scope Pre-school Curriculum Comparison study, validating the model's greater effectiveness relative to other competing models. Most countries adopting the High/Scope curriculum approach develop small local research studies to test issues of local adaptation.

A curriculum model needs to be used on a wide scale and in a wide range of settings to be certain that the system actually works. By necessity, a model is developed on a selected group of youngsters in a limited setting. But can a model that is well-implemented and effective on a limited scale replicate these features on a larger scale and with different populations? It is important to try the model out in a wide range of geographical locations, different language groups, varied ethnic clusters and selected ability groups to identify its adaptability or potential limitations when it is taken to scale.

For the High/Scope approach, research on the use of the method throughout the USA and many other countries has demonstrated its capacity and robust nature to assist children. National studies in the USA (Epstein, 1993) have shown that the model maintains its quality and fidelity in multiple replications. Other studies done in the United Kingdom by Carla Berry and Kathy Sylva (1987) and in Portugal by M. Nabuco and Kathy Sylva (1995) also give strength to the original work by examining the curriculum in other cultures, programme settings and language, *and socio-economic* groups.

Box 2. The High/Scope Training of Trainers Evaluation

The Training of Trainers (ToT) Evaluation investigated the efficacy of the High/Scope training and curriculum models for improving the quality of early childhood programmes on a national scale. In 1981, the High/Scope Educational Research Foundation in Ypsilanti, Michigan, embarked on the Training of Trainers initiative to provide in-service training to large numbers of early childhood practitioners throughout the country. As of 1991, High/Scope had conducted 80 ToT projects, producing 1,075 endorsed High/Scope trainers in 38 states and 12 other countries. These 1,075 trainers had, in turn, trained an estimated 26,000 teachers working with over a quarter of a million children annually.

Between 1989 and 1992 a multi-method evaluation was conducted to examine the effectiveness of the chain of transmission from the High/Scope consultant to the endorsed agency trainer to teachers to children. As part of this ambitious undertaking, High/Scope collected anecdotal records from the consultants and the 793 participants in 40 ToT projects, surveyed a random sample of 203 endorsed High/Scope trainers around the country, interviewed and observed teachers in 244 High/Scope and 122 non-High/Scope settings, and assessed 97 children in High/Scope and 103 children in comparison programmes.

In addition to the specific question of whether High/Scope's training is effective, the evaluation study also addressed the broader question of how in-service training can improve early childhood programme quality and enhance young children's development. Does in-service training, over and above a teacher's pre-service education and experience, improve the teacher's ability to deliver an appropriate and challenging programme to young children? And if it is possible to improve programme quality and child outcomes, then what can be learned about how training can be structured to bring about these positive results?

The study provided a strongly affirmative answer to the first question: High/Scope training does work. Programme sites around the country, separated from the High/Scope Foundation by both time and distance, were found to be implementing the High/Scope Curriculum at impressive levels of fidelity and quality. High/Scope sites significantly outscored comparison sites on a developmentally based index of programme quality. Children in High/Scope programmes significantly outscored those in comparison programmes on measures of development progress.

The research also provided strong evidence for the general assertion that in-service training can contribute significantly to programme quality and children's development. On-the-job training continues the process of professional development after formal education ceases. On-site learning helps teachers convert experience into improved practice, thereby enhancing programme quality. And better programme quality, in turn, facilitates sound child development.

Defining good in-service training

Clearly, in this time of rapid progress and change, preparing early childhood teachers to deliver good programmes must fall largely to in-service training methods.

The following characterictics are the features of the High/Scope approach to in-service training:

• ***Integrated content***. In-service training follows a progression of interrelated topics, resulting in knowledge that is cumulative over the course of training.

- **Presentation geared to adult learning**. Training procedures are based on current knowledge about how adults learn. Trainers interact with teachers during group workshop presentations and make individual on-site visits to the classroom for observation and feedback.

- **Articulated curriculum**. High/Scope has a coherent curriculum model based on child development principles. The curriculum serves as a framework for applying and implementing new knowledge.

- **Hands-on practice**. In-service training sessions explore strategies for practical application. Strategies are then practised in the actual work setting.

- **Distributive learning**. Training is spread out over many months, so staff alternate one week of workshop sessions with several weeks of application at their sponsoring agency. This cycle promotes adaptation and problem solving, and it highlights the progression of skills over time.

- **Follow-up mechanisms**. The regularity of training and supervision means that follow-up opportunities are built into the model. Trainees can explore issues individually with their trainer, as well as in group sessions with their peers.

Source: Epstein, A.S. 1993. Taken from *Training for quality: improving early childhood programmes through systematic in-service training*. Ypsilanti, MI: High/Scope Press, 1993, pp. xv, 6-7.

A validated training system

A model curriculum programme needs a validated training system, so that it can be transferred successfully from the model developers to a wide range of classrooms or care settings. Like the process needed to establish the validity of the model approach, developing an effective adult training programme to enable others to use the method is in the same order of difficulty. In a manner of speaking, an effective training programme must recapitulate all of the above steps. It needs to be based on a systematic model of effective adult learning. Simply disseminating the information about the model is not enough. It needs to be fully documented so that the training is consistent for all those learning the approach. If different trainers use different systems and information about the model, then the actual practice of the programme will be very different. It needs to be validated by research, so that the policy-makers applying the approach will know that the training component is effective. For the High/Scope approach, this validation step meant going into the field to interview High/Scope endorsed trainers, observe the individual teachers as they plan and implement the programme on a daily basis, and evaluate children in these settings to discover the extent of High/Scope curriculum impact (Epstein,1993). While validating the training model is difficult to undertake and complete, this final step is necessary for a model to go to scale and demonstrate its feasibility when widespread training can no longer be carried out directly by the programme developers. See the sidebar for a summary of High/Scope's training validation study.

A validated assessment system: child progress and programme implementation

A curriculum model needs an assessment system reliably indicating the growth achieved by participating children. Assessment systems are frequently selected to demonstrate child progress on dimensions that bear little or no relationship to the curriculum goals and methodology used. Typically, such systems are focused on narrow academic skills that are simple to measure, for example, using letter recognition as a measure of reading ability. In

75

general, such assessment instruments lack validity because they are artificial and do not provide a full picture of a child's motivations and abilities. These problems are especially true when assessment of pre-school children is undertaken. A good model will have an assessment plan that allows child progress to be monitored with an instrument that reflects the developmental intentions of the programme. The High/Scope approach uses the High/Scope Child Observation Record (1992), an observation system that allows adults to document progress in key cognitive and social development areas. As a documentation system, the findings are based on actual examples of behaviour that represent the best performance the child can spontaneously produce during the natural observation period. Recording these observations allows adults to plan activities that support and extend the abilities of the children in their programmes. Quantitative scores on the assessment instrument also indicate the success the approach has as it supports the child's growth.

A well-developed monitoring system must be available to ensure that the curriculum model is actually in operation when it is said to be employed. The final test of a model programme is whether or not it is actually in use. Often, curriculum models are more apparent in how adults describe their programme than in actual application. A model that is used to go to scale needs a system that allows independent observers to validate the fidelity of the actual programme implementation in daily operation. A well-designed programme monitoring scheme will also direct attention to areas in which adults need further training. In the High/Scope approach, the High/Scope Programme Quality Assessment (1998) is used for both monitoring and training purposes. This instrument allows any early-education programme to look at its quality of implementation, based on what is known from decades of research on best practices.

As outlined in *Figure 3*, a curriculum model designed to go to scale must meet very strict standards of validation. If large public expenditures are to be made for such an effort, the model must be able to offer assurance that its curriculum, training methods and assessment procedures are valid. Only then can policy-makers be assured that the model can be broadly implemented and achieve its promised effectiveness.

VII. Policy recommendations: contributions from early childhood development

In the past 40 or 50 years, early childhood has changed in its importance to public policy-makers. At one time, early childhood development was the responsibility of the family and received little input or interest from even the immediate community; now it is recognized as central to establishing character and success in adulthood. This change is the product of new circumstances for the family and from the startling information generated by decades-long studies examining intervention programmes. Patterns of child-care and education are changing as families throughout the world become more urban. As families seek jobs and a better life, their migration to the cities and suburbs is increasing. In many small, developing nations, over half the population lives in the capital city environs. This migration and drive for a better life is sending many more women into the paid workforce just at a time when support from the extended family is becoming less available. As seen in Chapter 2, the pattern is that the family generally enrols the young child in one or more care/education settings, with centre-based nursery care or an education programme being the most frequent choice. With rare exceptions, most families are satisfied with such arrangements. The need for care, coupled with the general satisfaction, makes it unlikely that this trend will be reversed. But what is the quality of that out-of-home care/education experience for children?

The answer to the quality question comes from longitudinal research. When such programmes meet essential high-quality standards, the results are impressive in benefits to children and their families as well as in benefits to the community at large. Children are better prepared to take advantage of later education opportunities and to participate as contributing members of society through their stable work roles and good citizenship. Of special importance is the fact that a major indicator of social dissatisfaction and personal anger – the number of arrests for criminal behaviour – is significantly reduced. Carefully obtained evidence also supports the public investment in high-quality early childhood programmes for disadvantaged children. These programmes return a substantial public taxpayer dividend of up to $7 on each $1 of operational cost *as documented in the High/Scope Perry study in the USA.*

The period from conception to school entry at age six or seven is a time of great development. Children begin life with a total dependency on those around them. The need for a significant caregiver is widely recognized as essential so that the child can form a primary attachment to a single person. Such a person, usually the mother, gives the emotional assurance through her care and feeding, through her presence and physical contact, and through her verbal reassurances that all is well and that fear and stressful situations will be alleviated. As indicated by the growing body of research on brain functioning, there are actual physical correlates to these functions of the caregiver. Normal development will not occur without such a relationship. While further research needs to be undertaken to define the parameters, it appears that the infant uses the time from birth to age two to develop the basic platforms of language, organizing sight and hearing, achieving internal physical functioning, gaining co-ordination of fundamental motor skills and forming the all-important attachment to a consistent and dependable caregiver. Research on programmes that attempt to accelerate these developmental processes or to introduce higher-order skills involving reading, writing or numbers have found limited immediate effects and no long-term impact.

The pre-school child, three to six years old, presents a very different picture in three ways. First, the child has language and develops new communication skills at a great rate. As a result, there is an increased ability to talk with new adults and peers with whom the child comes in contact. The willingness to use these emerging abilities reflects a growing comfort with and interest in people and things that are unfamiliar – this is the second change. Third, the child by now has developed extraordinary physical ability. No longer is this an infant who is restricted to looking at only what is in sight or grasping only what is within reach. Now having the ability to walk, the child can explore an increasingly greater area; having the capacity to use language, the child can accept new persons and in new situations can co-ordinate complex physical movements. The pre-school child is able to gain and express independence in word, thought and action.

Research on intervention programmes at this age records great success. However, the programmes are only successful when they are designed to meet the developmental ability of the child. Programmes that attempt to introduce functions from later stages of development or learning are ineffective. That is why studies such as the High/Scope Perry Pre-school study, which follow children over decades and into adulthood, record highly effective results. The effective programmes are ones that closely adhere to the developmental level of the child. They offer model curriculum approaches that permit the child to be actively involved with materials and other people (both adults and peers). They provide ample room and opportunity for the child to be physically active and engaged, and to explore events and things within the environment.

Based on the foregoing child development knowledge and programme research, successful early childhood programmes must meet the six criteria listed below.

1. **Use a well-defined and documented early childhood model curriculum approach that has been extensively validated.**

A number of early childhood programmes are the outcome of work over the last decades of intervention with disadvantaged children in the USA, Europe and many other areas of the world. It is tempting to think that some of these can be used as they are, adapted or amalgamated, or simply applied as thought expedient. However, as a programme is changed or as the population served differs, the programme moves further from its validated practices. Thus, the best model approaches serve as benchmarks as to what can be accomplished. If a new programme does not start from a model base, it risks starting at year one, or ground zero, instead of building on the back of decades of experience and carefully proven practice.

Recommendation for planners: Begin with a known model and work to make it valuable and applicable to the new programmes under consideration. Adapt the best models that focus on processes and not content. From what was seen in Chapter 3, child development differences in various ethnic and cultural settings are not as great as might be thought. Teachers and parents, when working with same-age children, hold many of the same opinions and objectives across many countries. A model curriculum, if valid, has universal application possibilities.

2. **Provide a systematic in-service training programme with ongoing supervision of curriculum practice by a trainer knowledgeable in the model employed and acquainted with the programme staff, children and parents involved.**

One of the more difficult ideas to grasp in early childhood education is that caregiver/teacher training must relate to the specific curriculum model used. It must be ongoing and on-site, and it must focus on the theories undergirding the approach and on application of the theories to the daily classroom practice. Training so often is organized around topics brought in from outside the programme framework, because they are thought to be useful or popular. However, when employing a model approach, all training should be built on the actual problems faced by the caregiver/staff in the application of the curriculum. Thus, for example, training sessions on parent involvement should focus on how to help parents facilitate their child's learning and activities at home, using an approach compatible with the model used in the classroom or centre.

Because the training needs to be connected with actual practice, it makes sense that training should be on-site and ongoing. Caregiver/staff need to experience training within the location and context of their work assignments. Doing training off-site in large centralized groups may be administratively efficient, but it breaks the tie to daily practice with specific children. Finally, there is always a temptation to add elements that the administrator, or even the trainer, believes to be attractive but that are from another theoretical point of view. A model curriculum is effective because it brings focus to the programme. By asking that inconsistent alternatives be ignored, the model greatly enables established effective practices to be implemented without interference or dilution.

Recommendation for policy planners: When selecting a curriculum methodology, the accompanying caregiver/staff-training programme is of equal importance. It needs to serve staff at their work site, be consistently delivered over time, and focus directly on the essential model curriculum practices. The training programme itself should present evidence that, when skilfully applied, it 'will deliver'. Not only should the model curriculum be validated as effective, but so should the training system.

3. **Pre-school children (ages three, four, five) learn best when there is one adult for about 8 to 10 children.**

In many countries, adults in early childhood care /education programmes are typically responsible for more children than recommended in this 1 to 8 or 10 ratio. Programmes with clear practices that the children understand may appear to work smoothly with larger numbers. However, with a large class the tendency for the adult is to direct it as a single group, rather than to permit child-initiated learning based on individual interests and abilities. From this tendency, other major impediments to learning for children begin to evolve, for example, lack of conversation with the adult, limited options for materials, significant waiting time with no engagement, developmental mismatch for individual children, and so on. Model curriculum practices can help to reduce such problems by giving, for example, suggestions for ways children can facilitate one another's involvement or for ways to include parent and community volunteers in classroom support roles. When smaller class sizes or lower adult-child ratios are not logistically or economically feasible, great thought must be given to compensating for the limitations to children's learning and initiative. These drawbacks cannot be just overlooked.

Recommendations for policy planners: While it may be impractical to reach a goal of one adult for 8 to 10 children, carefully selected valid model approaches offer ways to effectively reduce the problem while more permanent solutions are sought. Validated models, based on sound child development principles, offer strategies for maximizing children's active engagement in the learning process. They can minimize the risk that children will suffer from a lack of challenging interactions with materials, peers, and adults.

4. **Use validated assessment systems to judge child progress within the programme and to ensure that the model curriculum selected is actually in use.**

Probably the weakest area in implementing early childhood programmes is the area of assessment. Both classroom adults and parents are resistant to the use of child assessment, and many of the reasons for this resistance are correct. Many pre-school-level tests are inappropriate for various reasons. For example, the child's attention span is often limited when attention must be focused on what adults think is important, the child may not be feeling well on the day of the assessment, a formal test setting is not within the child's normal experience or expectations, or the adult giving the test is poorly trained. Yet programme operators and parents want to know how individual children are progressing, and programme funders and policy planners want to know if the programme is producing as expected from their investment. The solution is to use a child assessment that is based on direct observation of the child's performance. Observation instruments that the caregiver/staff can use in the classroom or centre give the clearest and most authentic picture of the child's progress. Organized around a developmental theoretical perspective, such instruments can be highly effective.

For judging programme implementation, observation is also recommended. Trained outside observers can quickly give a reliable estimate of the level of implementation by using scales developed to rate the model curriculum. Such ratings also give information about programme implementation areas that need strengthening. From this information, adult training can be organized and judgements made about the value of the programme. Most surveys of early childhood education/care programmes in the USA find a poor-to-modest level of programme quality. Careful assessment of known model curriculum programmes will indicate the steps necessary to achieve a high level of quality in early childhood services.

Recommendations for policy planners: Careful evaluation of child growth and development is important to staff, parents, and funders. It is important to devote resources to employing validated observation assessment tools. Through this method, it is possible to measure child progress, and assess children under natural programme circumstances. Such measures avoid the pitfalls of artificial assessment and genuinely reflect children's intentions and abilities.

Questions about the level of quality in a programme can be judged through systematic ratings of programme implementation. Therefore, to promote high-quality programmes, arrange for curriculum progress to be monitored using observation instruments completed by trained independent raters. The obtained information will provide a reasonable base to judge programme efficiency and direction for follow-up staff training activities. If a validated model curriculum is employed, the desired child development results can be obtained only when the programme reaches the required benchmarks of high-quality programme operation.

5. Active parent involvement is an essential part of the programme.

While it is unlikely that programmes to facilitate children's cognitive growth and development can be provided solely through parents, it is essential that parents be involved as much as possible. The limiting factors are the parents' work schedules and other responsibilities that may interfere with availability to participate. An ethical programme has parents involved. While teachers are the educational and child-development experts in the classroom, parents are the experts regarding the home, its values, their goals for the child, and community traditions. Teachers and parents need to work together.

Recommendations for policy planners: Parent involvement will take extra planning and training to accomplish smoothly. However, parent participation is essential for a programme to effectively reach the child and reflect local community values and customs. Parents and teachers should form a partnership to promote young children's development.

6. **Programmes need sufficient resources and good administration to operate effectively.**

Most model programmes that build around child-initiated learning require large quantities of materials for children to handle, explore, employ, and consume. An important advantage, however, is that these materials do not need to be commercially produced and purchased at high cost. They can be scrap or recycled materials (safe and clean) from industry, community, family, or farm. Indeed, fancy production toys and plastic materials are often limiting to the child's own ingenuity and imagination. But programmes do need sufficient resources to operate. Considerable thought needs to be given as to how these can be provided. In addition to lack of resources, good administration is often another missing component in an early education operation. Administrators are frequently loaded with other responsibilities and usually have little training in early childhood development. These key staff need special orientation and encouragement to support high-quality implementation of model curriculum programmes.

Recommendations for policy planners: The system of providing materials for early childhood programmes is often given low priority. This is a mistake, and strategies need to be in place to solve the problem as the programmes are developed. Caregiver/

staff should take advantage of the educational opportunities inherent in no-cost and low-cost items and invest the remaining resources in open-ended learning materials. Issues with administration are best resolved by initially assigning a skilled and sympathetic individual to such posts. While appointing an administrator is a decision that is only made once, it is a critical one to providing staff and caregivers with the support and understanding they need to implement the programme model effectively.

Challenging decisions

Policy-makers in every country are charged with the responsibility of establishing priorities for investing available resources. When a country is resource poor the challenge is even greater. What should have priority? Should building a base of better students, as in high-quality early childhood care/education, be emphasized and given more funds? Should primary education extend full coverage to both boys and girls in urban and rural areas? Should secondary school include more individuals and broaden the curriculum as well as lengthen the time? Limited resources demand careful consideration of expenditures. Where can investment get the most return? For the policy-maker none of these questions are easy nor are the answers obvious. What can be suggested from the research presented in this volume?

Recommendation for policy planners: A priority would be to ensure that the programmes already offered in early childhood care/education are of high quality. All countries in the international survey, regardless of their level of development, had extensive programmes for children under five. Ensuring these programmes meet high-quality standards would be a first priority. Money is already being spent to operate the programmes, including on the recruitment of children and the training of caregivers/staff. Of the four components necessary to create high-quality programmes – adequate health and safety standards, standards for training, qualifications of caregivers/staff, and comprehensive services – the most important is to adopt a model

85

curriculum programme which can be easily adapted to settings. A model programme allows limited funds to focus on clear-cut training and support to programmes to ensure their quality. It also reduces costs, since materials have already been developed for all three necessary components, the programme itself, the training material for staff, and the assessment of the children in the programme.

Early childhood programmes for children under five require the same consideration that programmes for primary and secondary schools demand. Each of these levels contributes to a different level of functioning by the child and, ultimately, to the health of the country itself. In the past, the early childhood care/education sector has been primarily overlooked as an important link in the development of an overall educational strategy within a country. As with all segments of education, incorporating special strategies to reduce programme costs without significant loss of quality is required. For example, as long as good training and supervision are provided, volunteers can work successfully in early childhood care/education programmes. This extra staff is especially important because the ratio of caregivers/ staff to participating children needs to be kept as high as possible. The standard recommendation is no more than one per ten for ages three, four and five.

Cost-benefit studies indicate that high-quality programmes produce better workers and better citizens; thus, early childhood care/ education programmes have moved to the centre of consideration for investment.

Final comments

Programme services for young children have grown out of recognition that early childhood is a time of beginnings and that working parents need help. From the research of the past several decades, it is now apparent that children set their life path during these years. While much can and should be offered to children as they grow into adulthood, these early years have the power to set in place the foundation for that growth. Over the years, the field has had the dedicated service of many individuals, usually women, who have sensed this power. It is only recently that the evidence has confirmed their commitment. However, like everything else in life, the quality of the experience is the key. Offering 'what we believe to be important for children' is no longer acceptable or sufficient. That commitment to **high quality** must be realized by building upon the best model curriculum approaches now available.

References

Barnett, W.S. 1995. "Long-term effects of early childhood programmes on cognitive and school outcomes". In: R.E. Behrman (Ed.), *The future of children: Long-term outcomes of early childhood programmes*, Vol. 5. No. 3, pp. 25-50, Winter. Los Altos, CA: The David and Lucille Packard Foundation.

Baumrind, D. 1971. "Current patterns of parental authority". In: *Developmental Psychology Monographs*, Vol. 4, No. 4, Part 2.

Berry, C.F.; Sylva, K. 1987. *The plan-do-review cycle in High/Scope: its effects on children and staff*. Oxford, Oxford University.

Bredekamp, S. (Ed.). 1987. *Developmentally appropriate practice in early childhood programmes serving children from birth through age 8*. Washington, D.C.: National Association for the Education of Young Children.

Bruer, J.T. 1997. "Education and the brain: a bridge too far". In: *Educational Researcher*, Vol. 26 (8), pp. 4-6.

Burts, D.C.; Hart, C.H.; Charlesworth, R.; Kirk, L. 1990. "A comparison of frequency of stress behaviours observed in kindergarten children in classrooms with developmentally appropriate versus developmentally inappropriate instructional practices". In: *Early Childhood Research Quarterly*, Vol. 5, pp. 407-423.

Burts, D.C.; Hart, C.H.; Charlesworth, R.; Fleege, P.O.; Mosley, J.; Thomasson, R.H. 1992. "Observed activities and stress behaviours of children in developmentally appropriate and inappropriate kindergarten classrooms". In: *Early Childhood Research Quarterly*, Vol. 7, pp. 297-318.

Cleverley, J.; Phillips, D.C. 1986. *Vision of childhood; influential models from Loche to Spock.* New York and London: Teachers College, Columbia University.

Cochran, M. (Ed.). 1993. *International handbook of child-care policies and programmes.* Westport, CT: Greenwood Press.

Datta, L.; McHale, C.; Mitchell, S. 1976. *The effects of Head Start classroom experience on some aspects of child development: a summary report of national evaluations*, 1966-69 DHEW Publication No. OHD-76-30088. Washington, D.C.: U S Government Printing Office.

DeVries, R.; Haney, J.P.; Zan, B. 1991. "Sociomoral atmosphere in direct-instruction, eclectic, and constructivist kindergartens: a study of teachers' enacted interpersonal understanding". Early Childhood Research Quarterly, Vol. 6, pp. 449-471.

DeVries, R.; Reese-Learned, H.; Morgan, P. 1991. "Sociomoral development in direct-instruction, eclectic, and constructivist kindergarten: a study of children's enacted interpersonal understanding". In: *Early Childhood Research Quarterly*, Vol. 6, pp. 473-517.

Donaldson, M. 1978. *Children's Minds.* London: Cromm Helm.

Epstein, A.S.; Weikart, D.P. 1979. *The Ypsilanti-Carnegie Infant Education Project: a longitudinal follow-up.* Ypsilanti, MI: High/Scope Press.

Epstein, A.S. 1993. *Training for quality: improving early childhood programmes through systematic in-service training.* Monographs of the High/Scope Educational Research Foundation, Vol. 9, pp. xv, 6-7. Ypsilanti, MI: High/Scope Press.

Frede, E.; Barnett, W.S. 1992. "Developmentally appropriate public school pre-school: a study of implementation of the High/Scope Curriculum and its effects on disadvantaged children's skills at first grade". In: *Early Childhood Research Quarterly*, Vol. 7, pp. 483-499.

Goffin, S.G. 1993. *Curriculum models and early childhood education: appraising the relationship.* New York, NY: Merrill.

High/Scope Educational Research Foundation. 1992. *The High/Scope Child Observation Record for ages 21/2 to 6.* Ypsilanti, MI: High/Scope Press.

High/Scope Educational Research Foundation. 1998. *The High/Scope Programme Quality Assessment: Pre-school version.* Ypsilanti, MI: High/Scope Press.

Hohmann, M.; Weikart, D.P. 1995. *Educating young children: Active learning practices for pre-school and child-care programmes.* Ypsilanti, MI: High/Scope Press.

Kagitcibari, Ç.; Sunar, D.; Bekman, S. 1988. *Comprehensive Pre-school Education Project: Final report.* Ottawa: International Development Research Centre.

Karnes, M.B.; Schwedel, A.M.; Williams, M.B. 1983. "A comparison of five approaches for educating young children from low-income homes". In: *Consortium for Longitudinal Studies, As the twig is bent ... Lasting effects of pre-school programmes*, pp. 133-170. Hillsdale, NJ: Erlbaum.

Kohlberg, L.; Mayer, R. 1972. "Development as the aim of education". Harvard Education Review, Vol. 42, No. 4, pp. 449-496.

Lambie, D.Z.; Bond, J.T.; Weikart, D.P. 1974. *Home teaching with mothers and infants: The Ypsilanti-Carnegie Infant Education Project – An experiment.* Monographs of the High/Scope Educational Research Foundation, 2. Ypsilanti, MI: High/Scope Press.

Larner, M.; Halpern, R.; Harkavy, O. 1992. *Fair start for children: lessons learned from several demonstration projects.* New Haven, CT: Yale University Press.

Lazar, I.; Darlington, R.; Murray, H.; Royce, J.; Snipper, A. 1982. *Lasting effects of early education: a report from the Consortium for Longitudinal Studies.* Monographs of the Society for Research in Child Development, Vol. 47 (2-3, Serial No. 195).

Marcon, R.A. 1992. "Differential effects of three pre-school models on inner-city 4-year-olds". In: *Early Childhood Research Quarterly*, Vol. 7, pp. 517-530.

Marcon, R.A. 1994. "Doing the right thing for children: linking research and policy reform in the District of Columbia public schools". In: *Young Children*, Vol. 50(1), 8-20, November.

McKey, R.H.; Condelli, L.; Ganson, H.; Barrett, B.J.; McConkey, C.; Plantz, M.C. 1985. *The impact of Head Start on children, families, and communities* – Final report of the Head Start Evaluation, Synthesis, and Utilization Project. Washington, D.C.: CSR.

Miller, L.B.; Bizzell, R.P. 1983. "The Louisville experiment: a comparison of four programmes". In: *Consortium for Longitudinal Studies, As the twig is bent ... Lasting effects of pre-school programmes*, pp. 171-199. Hillsdale, NJ: Erlbaum.

Myers, R. 1992. *The twelve who survive: strengthening programmes of early childhood development in the Third World.* London: Routledge; Paris: UNESCO.

Nabuco, M.; Sylva, K. 1995. *Comparisons between ECERS ratings of individual pre-school centres and the results of target child observations: do they match or do they differ?* Paper presented to the 5th European Conference on the Quality of Early Childhood Education, Paris.

Olmstedt, P.P.; Weikart, D.P. (Eds.). 1989. *How nations serve young children: profiles of child-care and education in 14 countries.* Ypsilanti, MI: High/Scope Press.

Olmstedt, P.P.; Weikart, D.P. (Eds.). 1994. *Families speak: early childhood care and education in 11 countries.* Ypsilanti, MI: High/Scope Press.

Onibokun, O. 1989. "Early childhood care and education in Nigeria". In: *How nations serve young children: profiles of child-care and education in 14 countries*, pp. 219-240. Olmstedt, P.P.; Weikart, D.P. (Eds.). Ypsilanti, MI: High/Scope Press.

Osborn, D.K. 1991. *Early childhood education in historical perspective.* Athens, GA: Daye Press.

Ramey, C.T.; Bryant, D.M.; Suarez, T.M. 1985. "Pre-school compensatory education and modifiability of intelligence: a critical review". In: D. Detterman (Ed.), *Current topics in intelligence*, pp. 247-296. Norwood, NJ: Ablex.

Schweinhart, L.J.; Barnes, H.V.; Weikart, D.P., with Barnett, W.S.; Epstein, A.S. 1993. *Significant benefits: the High/Scope Perry Pre-school study through age 27.* Monographs of the High/Scope Educational Research Foundation, 10. Ypsilanti, MI: High/Scope Press.

Schweinhart, L.J.; Weikart, D.P. 1997. *Lasting differences: the High/Scope Pre-school Curriculum Comparison study through age 23.* Monographs of the High/Scope Educational Research Foundation, 12. Ypsilanti, MI: High/Scope Press.

Shi Hui Zhong. 1989. "Young children's care and education in the People's Republic of China". In: *How nations serve young children: profiles of child-care and education in 14 countries*, pp. 241-254. Olmstedt, P.P.; Weikart, D.P. (Eds.). Ypsilanti, MI: High/Scope Press.

St. Pierre, R.G.; Layzer, J.I.; Barnes, H.V. 1995. "Two-generation programmes: design, cost, and short-term effectiveness". In: R.E. Behrman (Ed.), *The future of children: Long-term outcomes of early childhood programmes*, Vol. 5, No. 3, pp. 77-93, Winter. Los Altos, CA: The David and Lucille Packard Foundation.

United Nations Educational, Scientific, and Cultural Organization (UNESCO). 1989. *1988 World Survey on Early Childhood Care and Education (ECCE): Summary of findings*. Paris: UNESCO.

Walsh, D.J.; Smith, M.E.; Alexander, M.; Ellwein, M.C. 1993. "The curriculum as mysterious and constraining: teachers' negotiations of the first year of a pilot programme for at-risk 4-year-olds". In: *Journal of Curriculum Studies*, Vol. 25, pp. 317-332.

Weikart, D.P. 1972. "Relationship of curriculum, teaching, and learning in pre-school education". In: J. C. Stanley (Ed.), *Pre-school programmes for the disadvantaged*. Baltimore, MD: John Hopkins University Press.

Weikart, D.P. (Ed.). 1999. *What should young children learn? Teacher and parent views in 15 countries*. Ypsilanti, MI: High/Scope Press.

IIEP publications and documents

More than 1,200 titles on all aspects of educational planning have been published by the International Institute for Educational Planning. A comprehensive catalogue is available in the following subject categories:

Educational planning and global issues
General studies – global/developmental issues

Administration and management of education
Decentralization – participation – distance education – school mapping – teachers

Economics of education
Costs and financing – employment – international co-operation

Quality of education
Evaluation – innovation – supervision

Different levels of formal education
Primary to higher education

Alternative strategies for education
Lifelong education – non-formal education – disadvantaged groups – gender education

Copies of the Catalogue may be obtained on request from:
IIEP, Dissemination of Publications
information@iiep.unesco.org
Titles of new publications and abstracts may be consulted at the
following website: *http://www.unesco.org/iiep*

The International Institute for Educational Planning

The International Institute for Educational Planning (IIEP) is an international centre for advanced training and research in the field of educational planning. It was established by UNESCO in 1963 and is financed by UNESCO and by voluntary contributions from Member States. In recent years the following Member States have provided voluntary contributions to the Institute: Denmark, Germany, Iceland, India, Ireland, Norway, Sweden, Switzerland and Venezuela.

The Institute's aim is to contribute to the development of education throughout the world, by expanding both knowledge and the supply of competent professionals in the field of educational planning. In this endeavour the Institute co-operates with interested training and research organizations in Member States. The Governing Board of the IIEP, which approves the Institute's programme and budget, consists of a maximum of eight elected members and four members designated by the United Nations Organization and certain of its specialized agencies and institutes.

Inquiries about the Institute should be addressed to:
The Office of the Director, International Institute for Educational Planning,
7-9 rue Eugène-Delacroix, 75116 Paris, France.

$\cdots$ SAGIM $\cdots$

Achevé d'imprimer en décembre 2000
sur les presses de l'imprimerie
SAGIM à Courtry (77)

Imprimé en France

Dépôt légal : décembre 2000
N° d'impression : 4824

DATE DUE